Job Control Language

2nd Edition

D1558311

Related Books from the Wiley Press

ANS COBOL, 2nd ed., Ashley
COBOL for Microcomputers, Ashley and Fernandez
Structured COBOL, Ashley
The Complete FORTH, Winfield
Fortran IV, 2nd ed., Friedmann, Greenberg and Hoffberg

Job Control Language

2nd Edition

Ruth Ashley
Judi N. Fernandez

Co-Presidents, DuoTech

A WILEY PRESS BOOK

John Wiley & Sons, Inc.

New York • Chichester • Brisbane • Toronto • Singapore

Publisher: Judy V. Wilson
Editor: Theron Shreve
Managing Editor: Katherine Schowalter
Composition and Make-up: Editing, Design & Production, Inc.

Library of Congress Cataloging in Publication Data

Ashley, Ruth.
    Job control language.

    (Wiley self-teaching guides)
    "A Wiley Press book."
    Includes index.
    1. Job Control Language (Computer program language)—
Programmed instruction.   2. Electronic digital computers
—Programming—Programmed instruction.   I. Fernandez,
Judi N.   II. Title.   III. Series: Self-teaching guide.
QA76.73.J63A78   1983   001.64′24   83-16855
ISBN 0-471-79983-1

1984   1985   10 9 8 7 6 5 4 3 2 1

Acknowledgments

It takes many people to help produce a book like this—the folks at Wiley, our technical consultants and reviewers, numerous typists, typesetters, artists, and so forth. For this second edition, we would particularly like to acknowledge the excellent technical revisions suggested by Gabe Gargiulo.

Contents

viii CONTENTS

To the Reader

About JCL

Job Control Language allows a programmer or operator to communicate with an IBM operating system. Without JCL to serve as the interface, you can't get the IBM operating system to run a program. The JCL presented in this Self-Teaching Guide is specifically applicable to the following systems.

360	OS/MFT	
	OS/MVT	
370 and compatible machines	OS/VS1	
	OS/VS2	SVS
		MVS

Notes are added in the text wherever the information, as presented, is different for any of the above systems.

This Guide does not include all the JCL there is, even for these systems. It will, however, give you the skill and knowledge to function competently in an environment that requires JCL. You will not be merely copying "control cards," but devising your own so that you, as programmer or operator, can actually control what the operating system is doing with your job. When you finish your study of this Guide, you will be at ease with the language of JCL, and you will be easily able to learn more from local installation documentation or the ubiquitous IBM manuals. The productivity of an application programmer increases greatly when a facility with JCL is added to knowledge of a high-level language.

About the Authors Versus JCL

The authors of this Guide used the various high-level languages for years before learning JCL. We copied "control cards," or handed over our programs for someone else to run. We believed the prevalent rumors that JCL was horrible, and only "die-hard" computer-types ever understood it. But then, in self-defense, we suddenly *had* to learn to use JCL. And we discovered what JCL can do—liberate you from the defaults and "usual usage" of your installation. It allows you to control what the system does with your job. And it wasn't impossible after all! In this Guide, we allow you to benefit from our trauma, as we have applied the time-honored techniques of instructional technology to make it easy for you to learn the basics and applications of Job Control Language.

Ruth Ashley
Judi Fernandez

How to Use This Book

This Self-Teaching Guide consists of eight chapters, each bringing you deeper into Job Control Language, building on the previous information. Each chapter begins with a short introduction, followed by objectives that outline what you can expect to learn from that chapter. And each chapter ends with a Summary Exercise, which allows you to test whether you have learned the material. In almost every case, the Summary Exercise is a complete job for you to code.

The body of each chapter is divided into frames—short numbered sections in which information is presented or reviewed, followed by questions which ask you to apply the information. The correct answers to these questions follow a dashed line after the frame. As you work through the Guide, use a folded paper or punch card to cover the correct answer until you have written yours. And be sure you actually write each response, especially when the activity is statement coding. Only by actually coding JCL statements, and checking them carefully (letter by letter, space by space) can you get the most from this Self-Teaching Guide.

On page 149, you will find a Glossary to the technical words used in the text; this is not exhaustive or all-inclusive. It will serve, however, to give fairly precise definitions to terms with which you may not be familiar.

Prerequisites

Very few people will ever begin studying computers or data processing with JCL. For this reason, we have assumed that you, the reader, have a knowledge of basic data processing. You know generally what computers can do, and you can program, at least somewhat, in a high-level language such as FORTRAN, COBOL, or PL/I. You probably also know something about operating systems and hardware devices for files or data sets. An intensive knowledge of these subjects is not required, but some degree of familiarity will enable you to work through this Self-Teaching Guide in comfort and develop some skills in JCL.

chapter one

Basic JCL Concepts

The large-scale IBM computers (actually, almost all computers) have operating systems. An operating system maintains control over what the computer does. To run a program, you request the operating system to transfer control to your program. When your program ends (normally or abnormally), the operating system takes back control and goes on to the next request.

The operating system is itself a set of programs, much of which is locked into the machine's storage. It can be thought of as a large control program that invokes other programs; each program executed is like a subprogram to the operating system.

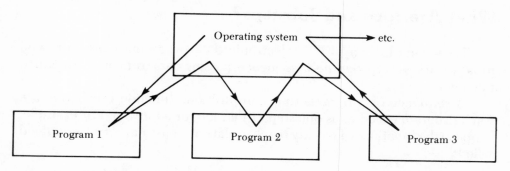

Note: The large-scale IBM machines have a variety of operating systems available to them. Your installation will have purchased the one that best meets its needs. Each operating system speaks a variation of JCL; that is, each one has some entries that are unique. This book deals with the most commonly used IBM operating systems—OS and MVS. The basic principles will also be useful to JCL for other operating systems, but some of the details may not be.

JCL is a computer language. Like COBOL or FORTRAN, it has a specific syntax and vocabulary. In this introductory chapter, you will become oriented to the major features of JCL, some important terminology, and two jobs that we will use throughout the book—and that you will probably use for many years to come.

When you have completed this chapter, you will be able to

- Recognize and apply these terms: job; jobstep; data set; system messages; parameter; positional parameter; keyword parameter; subparameter; system default
- Given a system flow diagram, identify the JCL statements that are needed to accomplish the job, in correct order
- Create a valid jobname, stepname, and ddname
- Code the beginning of a JCL statement on a coding form (up through column 16)
- Indicate to the system that a JCL statement is continued
- Include comments in JCL code
- Indicate how to invoke a system default
- Indicate how to override a system default
- Given the format for a parameter, code the parameter for a specific application

Appendix A is an additional description of what JCL is and how you use it. You might want to read that appendix now.

What Are Jobs and Jobsteps?

1. To accomplish any EDP (electronic data processing) function, you usually run several programs in sequence, passing data from one program to the next.

A sequence of programs to accomplish one function is called a *job*. Each program executed is one step of that job, or a *jobstep*. For example, suppose the function is a weekly batch update of a customer file, as outlined below.

(1) Sort the update records into ascending numerical sequence of account number and put the sorted file on disk.

(2) Use this file on disk to update the customer file.

(3) Use the updated customer file to prepare a management report.

The system flow diagram would look like the one at the top of page 3.

(a) How many jobs are shown in this example? _____

(b) How many jobsteps? _____

- - - - - - - - - -

(a) 1; (b) 3

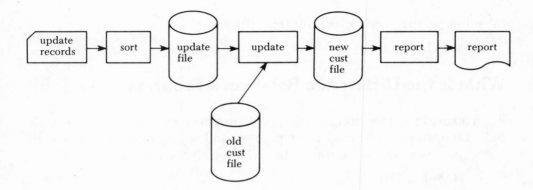

2. Here is another example of jobs and jobsteps. Suppose you have written an application program in a high-level language such as COBOL, and now you want to compile it, link edit it, and test it, all in one run.

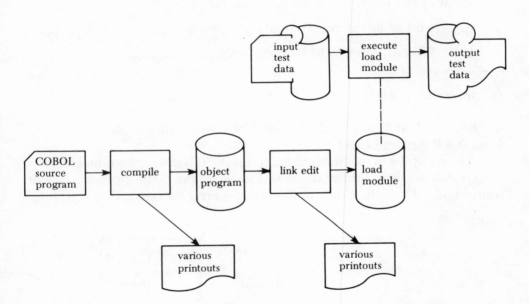

   This is a very important function, and one which we will use throughout this book. It is usually called "Compile, Link, and Go." "Go" means to execute or run the load module (executable program).

   For now we are concerned only with jobs and jobsteps. Label each of the following as job or jobstep.

   (a)   Compile_____

   (b)   Link edit_____

   (c)   Execute load module (Go)_____

   (d)   Compile, Link, and Go_____

- - - - - - - - - -

(a) jobstep; (b) jobstep; (c) jobstep; (d) job

What Is the Difference Between a Program and a Job?

3.   You are used to writing programs. A program is a series of instructions telling the computer how to input, process, and output data. In JCL, we do not write programs; we define jobs. JCL says (very briefly):

- Here is a job.

- For the first step, execute program A.

- For the second step, execute program B.

- For the third step, execute program C.

Identify the following as program or JCL job.

(a)   A list of instructions on data processing_____

(b)   A list of jobsteps to be executed_____

- - - - - - - - - -

(a) program; (b) job

4.   Let's look at Compile, Link, and Go in terms of programs and jobs. Examine the chart below.

The compiler in the first step is a *program*. It is usually supplied by IBM (and purchased by your installation). The input data to the program is your source code. The output data is object code, error messages, and warnings.

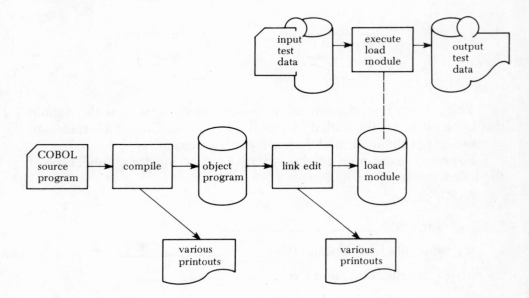

What about the rest of the parts of the system flow diagram—can you tell whether they are programs or jobs? Label each of the following.

(a) Instructions to the operating system to first execute the compiler, then the link editor, then the load module._____

(b) The link editor_____

(c) The load module_____

- - - - - - - - - -

(a) job; (b) program; (c) program

What Is a Data Set?

5. In JCL, we don't talk about files; we talk about *data sets*. Some experts say there is no difference between a file and a data set. Others claim that there is a difference, that there are some data sets that are not files. Regardless, we will use the term *data sets* to refer to the files used in a job.
Indicate when each term is used.

_____ (a) Files   A. Application programs

_____ (b) Data sets   B. JCL jobs

- - - - - - - - - -

(a) A; (b) B

6. In the first frame in this chapter, you identified three jobsteps in the job shown below.

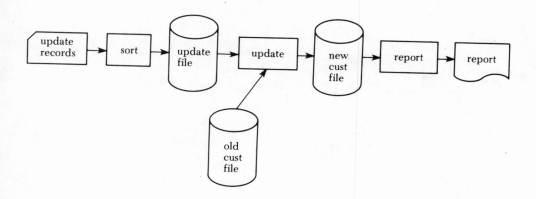

Now list the data sets associated with each jobstep.

JOBSTEP 1: SORT	JOBSTEP 2: UPDATE	JOBSTEP 3: REPORT

- - - - - - - - - -

JOBSTEP 1: SORT	JOBSTEP 2: UPDATE	JOBSTEP 3: REPORT
update records update file	update file old cust file new cust file	new cust file report

7. See if you can do a complete list of the data sets needed for the Compile, Link, and Go job. (The system flow diagram is more specific here to allow you to identify data sets.) Caution: The load module is an output data set in one step, but it is the program being executed in the next. The load module is never an input data set.

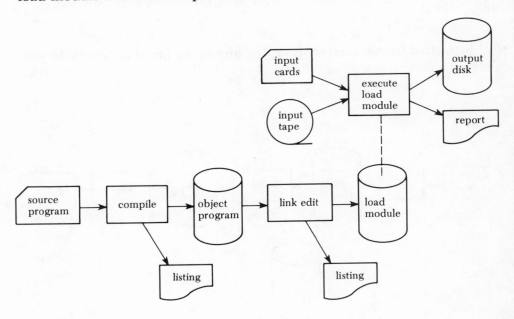

JOBSTEP 1: COMPILE	JOBSTEP 2: LINK EDIT	JOBSTEP 3: GO

- - - - - - - - - -

JOBSTEP 1: COMPILE	JOBSTEP 2: LINK EDIT	JOBSTEP 3: GO
source program object program	object program load module	input cards input tape output disk report

The Structure of JCL

8.   JCL is made up of *statements*. There are only nine types of statements. Three of them are necessary to every job:

JOB
This statement must be the first statement in every job; it signals the beginning of the job and therefore the end of the previous job. It contains important information about the job such as whom to charge it to, who the responsible programmer is, maximum CPU time, what hardware configuration the job requires, and so on.

EXEC
This statement identifies each jobstep and tells the operating system what program or procedure to EXECute. It may also include maximum CPU time for the step, hardware configuration for the step, whom to charge the step to (if not the same as the job), under what conditions to skip the step, and so on.

DD
Each Data Definition statement identifies one data set needed for the jobstep. The DD statement tells where to find the data set, what to do with it at the end of the jobstep, and so on. One DD statement is needed for every data set.

Refer back to the example in frame 7. How many of each type of statement are needed?

(a)   JOB_____

(b) EXEC_____

(c) DD_____

- - - - - - - - - -

(a) 1; (b) 3; (c) 10

9.   The statements in JCL must appear in a specific sequence. The JOB statement must come first, followed by the EXEC statement for the first jobstep. This must be immediately followed by all the DD statements for that jobstep, in any order. Then comes the EXEC statement for the next jobstep, its DD statements, and so on.

Refer back to the example in frame 7. Number the JCL statements shown below in the proper order.

_____ (a) EXEC load module

_____ (b) { DD object program / DD load module / DD listing

_____ (c) JOB

_____ (d) EXEC compile

_____ (e) EXEC link edit

_____ (f) { DD input cards / DD input tape / DD output tape / DD report

_____ (g) { DD source deck / DD object program / DD listing

- - - - - - - - - -

(a) 6; (b) 5; (c) 1; (d) 2; (e) 4; (f) 7; (g) 3

10.   Every JCL statement may be named. The JOB statement must have a jobname. The EXEC statement may have a stepname. The DD statement, in almost every case, must have a ddname. For example, in the Compile, Link, and Go job, the JOB statement may be named COLINKGO; the first EXEC statement may be named COMPSTEP; the first DD statement may be named SYSIN.

The same general rules apply to the formation of simple names of all three types:

- Each name must be unique within the job or jobstep.

- Names may be up to eight characters long.

- Names may include letters, digits, and $, @, or # (no spaces or hyphens).

- The first character may not be a digit.

(a) What type of name is included in the first statement for a job?

_____ Is it required? _____

(b) What type of name is included in each EXEC statement?

_____ Is it required? _____

(c) What type of name is included in a DD statement?

_____ Is it required? _____

(d) Indicate which of the names below are correctly formed according to the rules given above.

_____ A. P700   _____ E. 27THSTEP

_____ B. DATASET1   _____ F. UPDATE

_____ C. STEPSEVEN   _____ G. TRO6P975

_____ D. $498   _____ H. STEP-#7

- - - - - - - - - -

(a) jobname, yes
(b) stepname, no
(c) ddname, yes (in almost every case)
(d) A, B, D, F, G (C is too long; E begins with a digit; H includes a hyphen, one of the characters not allowed)

IBM Rules vs. Local Naming Conventions

Your installation may have additional rules pertaining to the formation of JCL names. For example, they may want you to use department codes as part of the names or to use meaningful abbreviations. In this book, we will always try to use meaningful abbreviations on the assumption that JCL must be used and understood by more than one person.

JCL Coding

11. On the following page is an 80-column coding form, which may be used to write JCL statements. We'll use this form to demonstrate the correct format of JCL code.

When coding JCL statements, you begin each line with two slashes (in columns 1 and 2). The name begins in column 3. This is followed by one or

1	2	3	4	5	6	7	8	9	10	11	12	13	14	15	16	17	18	19	20	21	22	23	24	25	26	27	28	29	30	31	32	33	34	35	36	37	38	39	40	41	42	43	44	45	46	47	48	49	50	51	52	53	54	55	56	57	58	59	60	61	62	63	64	65	66	67	68	69	70	71	72	73	74	75	76	77	78	79	80

more spaces. Then comes the keyword for the type of statement—JOB, EXEC, or DD—again followed by one or more spaces. Finally comes the information section of the statement. So the general format of a JCL statement is:

// name   type information

The code below shows the first part of each JCL statement for the first jobstep in an update job.

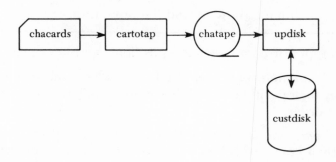

| 1 2 3 4 5 6 7 8 9 10 11 12 13 14 15 16 17 18 19 20 21 22 23 24 25 26 27 28 29 30 31 32 33 34 35 36 37 38 39 40 41 42 43 44 45 46 47 48 49 50 |
```
//CUSTUP   JOB
//CARTOTAP EXEC
//CHACARDS DD
//CHATAPE  DD
```

Write the first part of each JCL statement for the second step as shown in the flow diagram. Note that CHATAPE is an input file for the second step.

- - - - - - - - - -

| 1 2 3 4 5 6 7 8 9 10 11 12 13 14 15 16 17 18 19 20 21 22 23 24 25 26 27 28 29 30 31 32 33 34 35 36 37 38 39 40 41 42 43 44 45 46 47 48 49 50 |
```
//UPDISK   EXEC
//CHATAPE  DD
//CUSTDISK DD
```

12.   The information for each statement is contained in one or more *parameters*. The following chart shows some examples of parameters.

JOB	Accounting info (who to charge computer time to) Programmer's name Time (maximum CPU time allowed for the job)
EXEC	Name of program or procedure to be executed Time (maximum CPU time allowed for the step) Region (how much internal storage needed for the step)
DD	Unit (what hardware unit the data set needs) Space (how much room a disk file needs) Volume (how to find the tape or disk)

The two types of parameters are positional and keyword.

Positional parameters are identified and understood by the operating system by their position in the JCL statement. They must be coded in a specified order.

Keyword parameters are identified and understood by the operating system by a keyword followed by an equal sign. They need not be coded in any special order.

Here is a sample statement showing both types of parameters.

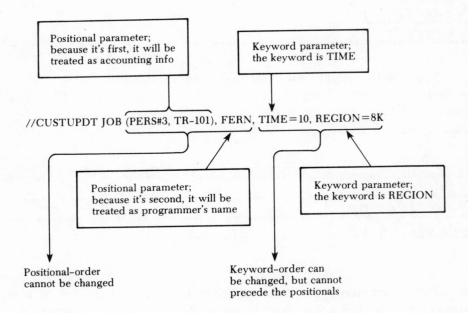

Notice that commas act as separators, and no blanks are used between parameters.

(a) Match the following.

_____ (1) Identified and understood   A. positional
             by presence of a keyword   B. keyword

_____ (2) Identified and understood
             by position

_____ (3) Identified by the equal sign (=)

(b) Label the indicated parameters as keyword or positional.

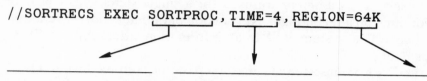

```
//SORTRECS EXEC SORTPROC,TIME=4,REGION=64K
```

(c) What character is used to separate parameters?_____

— — — — — — — — — —

(a) (1) B; (2) A; (3) B
(b) Positional, keyword, keyword
(c) Comma

13. Sometimes a parameter has more than one part; each part is called a subparameter. Here is an example:

$$TIME=(4,30),REGION=8K$$

> Positional subparameters;
> 4 means 4 minutes,
> 30 means 30 seconds.

Parentheses are used to group subparameters together to make one parameter. Commas act as separators both inside and outside the parentheses. Most subparameters are positional; you will study a few exceptions later.

Here is the format for one DD parameter, DISP, which specifies the disposition of the data set.

$$DISP = (\begin{Bmatrix} NEW \\ OLD \end{Bmatrix} , \begin{Bmatrix} KEEP \\ DELETE \end{Bmatrix} , \begin{Bmatrix} KEEP \\ DELETE \end{Bmatrix})$$

This first subparameter tells whether the data set already exists (OLD) or will be created by this step (NEW). The second subparameter tells whether to keep or delete the data set at the successful end of the jobstep. The third subparameter tells what to do with the data set if the jobstep abends. The braces are not coded but indicate that you may select one of the enclosed subparameters. The parentheses are coded in most cases. Write a DISP parameter for an input data set that should be deleted if the step is successful but kept if the step abends.

– – – – – – – – – –

DISP=(OLD,DELETE,KEEP)

14.   When several parameters are used for a single statement, you may need to continue on a second line. Never code parameters beyond column 71 on a line. (The system will treat information after column 71 as comments only.)

Always divide your statement after a separating comma. Leave at least one blank following the comma. (The blank may fall in column 72, but the comma may not.)

On the second line, and all subsequent lines, place // in the first two columns and continue with the next parameter or subparameter starting anywhere in columns 4–16.

(a)   What is the last column in which you can code parameter information?_____

(b)   Where should you divide a JCL statement?

_____ (1) After the name field

_____ (2) After any parameter and its comma

_____ (3) After any subparameter and its comma

(c)   What two features are needed in a continuation line (that is, the second line)?_____

(d)   Assume that a programmer formatted the following JOB statement incorrectly. Recode it so that the system will read it properly.

– – – – – – – – – –

(a) 71

(b) 2,3

(c) //; begin in columns 4–16

(d) Your coding should have these characteristics:
Statement divided after comma
Not coded beyond column 71
Continuation lines sta⁺ with //
Continuation parameters start in columns 4–16
Here is an example of a correct answer:

```
| 1| 2| 3| 4| 5| 6| 7| 8| 9|10|11|12|13|14|15|16|17|18|19|20|21|22|23|24|25|26|27|28|29|30|31|32|33|34|35|36|37|38|39|40|41|42|43|44|45|
//WRONGJOB JOB  (PERS#3,TR-101),ABIGAILVANDER
```

```
|46|47|48|49|50|51|52|53|54|55|56|57|58|59|60|61|62|63|64|65|66|67|68|69|70|71|72|73|74|75|76|77|78|79|80|
      SMITH,TIME=(100,30),
```

```
| 1| 2| 3| 4| 5| 6| 7| 8| 9|10|11|12|13|14|15|16|17|18|19|20|21|22|23|24|25|26|27|28|29|30|31|32|33|34|35|36|37|38|39|40|41|42|43|44|45|
//       REGION=128K,COND=(0,NE),CLASS=A
```

15. Comments may be included in your JCL code. Anything you wish can be included: explanations, sequence numbers, or program identifications. You may add comments to any JCL line after the last space. You can code comments all the way out through column 80. Examples:

```
//UPDATER  JOB  (PERS#3,TR-101),JONES  COMMENTS HERE
//SPECPROC EXEC PGM=PROCRJTS,TIME=4    COMMENTS HERE
//            REGION=64K COMMENTS MAY BE CODED HERE
```

There are two ways to code a whole line of comments.

- Put // in columns 1 and 2; leave 3–16 blank; put your comments in columns 17–80 (most people do not use this method).

- Put //* in columns 1–3; leave 4 blank; code your comments in columns 5–80 (this is the preferred method).

(a) What type(s) of JCL statement can include comments?

_____

(b) On the following lines, mark where comments could be placed.

```
| 1| 2| 3| 4| 5| 6| 7| 8| 9|10|11|12|13|14|15|16|17|18|19|20|21|22|23|24|25|26|27|28|29|30|31|32|33|34| |65|66|67|68|69|70|71|72|73|74|75|76|77|78|79|80|
//INTAPE   DD   DCB=(BLKSIZE=1000,)
//     LRECL=100,RECFM=FB),
//     DISP=(OLD,DELETE)
//*
```

(c) Which of the following would be treated as comments?

_____ (1) //   JOB   (PERS#3,TR-101),
             //   SMITH

_____ (2) //* THIS JOB WILL CREATE A FILE NAMED
             //   NEWSKILLS

_____ (3) Neither of the preceding

- - - - - - - - - - -

(a) All types

(b)

(c) 1,2

16. The flow diagram below represents a two-step job named EXAMPLE2. Stepnames and ddnames are shown on the diagram. Write the first part (through column 16) for each JCL statement that would be needed to run this job. Assume each EXEC statement will take two lines. Include the beginning of the continuation lines also; code an X to show in which column you would start coding the parameters in each continuation line.

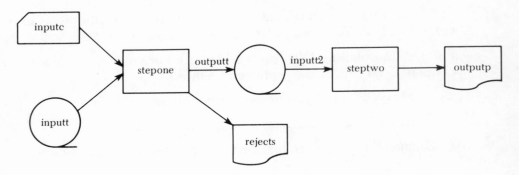

1	2	3	4	5	6	7	8	9	10	11	12	13	14	15	16	17	18	19	20	21	22	23	24	25	26	27	28	29	30	31	32	33	34	35	36	37	38	39	40	41	42	43	44	45	46	47	48	49	50

- - - - - - - - - -

1	2	3	4	5	6	7	8	9	10	11	12	13	14	15	16	17	18	19	20	21	22	23	24	25	26	27	28	29	30	31	32

```
//EXAMPLE2 JOB
//STEPONE  EXEC
//  XXXXXXXXXXXXXX
//INPUTC   DD
//INPUTT   DD
//OUTPUTT  DD
//REJECTS  DD
//STEPTWO  EXEC
//  XXXXXXXXXXXXX
//INPUTT2  DD
//OUTPUTP  DD
```

(Your X could be in any column from 4 through 16.)

System Defaults

17. IBM provides defaults for many JCL parameters. For example, if you omit the TIME parameter from the JOB statement, the system will fill in 30 minutes. However, your installation may have changed IBM's default values. So, your installation may have a TIME default of 10 minutes.

It is very important that you find out what the default values are at your installation:

– So you can omit parameters when you want to use the default value;

– So you can include parameters when you want to override the default values.

Your installation may not permit you to override default values without special permission.

(a) Suppose your installation has included a TIME default of 10 minutes. You want to use the 10-minute time maximum. What should you do?

_____ (1) Code TIME=10

_____ (2) Omit the TIME parameter

_____ (3) Either of the above will do

(b) Suppose you want to use a 5-minute time limit. What should you do?

_____ (1) Code TIME=5

_____ (2) Omit the TIME parameter

_____ (3) Either of the above will do

- - - - - - - - - -

(a) 3; (b) 1

Summary Exercises

```
//UPDATE EXEC COMPLK,TIME=(4,10),REGION=156K
```

1. Refer to the JCL statement above. Identify:
   (a) A keyword parameter_____
   (b) A positional parameter_____
   (c) A parameter with subparameters_____

2. Refer to the JCL statement above. What sort of name is UPDATE?

   _____

3. Name the type of JCL statement that:
   (a) Tells the operating system that a new job is beginning

   _____

   (b) Tells the operating system that a new jobstep is beginning

   _____

   (c) Describes a data set to the operating system_____

4. Assume that the computer system normally allows a default storage capacity of 64K bytes per job. Identify which of the following parameters will be used for the conditions below.

(1)   Don't code a region parameter
(2)   REGION=32K
(3)   REGION=64K

(a)   Which parameter will specify maximum storage of 32K?_____

(b)   Which will specify that the job needs 64K?_____

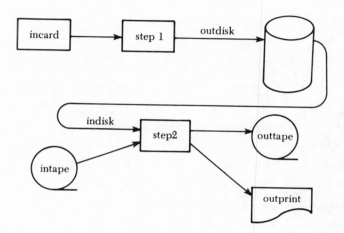

5.   The system flow diagram above represents a job named SAMPLE. Write the first part of each JCL statement needed in the correct order. The DD statement for OUTDISK will require two lines, so show the continuation.

| 1 | 2 | 3 | 4 | 5 | 6 | 7 | 8 | 9 | 10 | 11 | 12 | 13 | 14 | 15 | 16 | 17 | 18 | 19 | 20 | 21 | 22 | 23 | 24 | 25 | 26 | 27 | 28 | 29 | 30 | 31 | 32 | 33 | 34 | 35 | 36 | 37 | 38 | 39 | 40 | 41 | 42 | 43 | 44 | 45 | 46 | 47 | 48 | 49 | 50 |

Answers to Summary Exercises

1. (a) TIME or REGION; (b) COMPLK; (c) TIME
2. Stepname
3. (a) JOB; (b) EXEC; (c) DD
4. (a) 2; (b) 1 or 3
5.

```
1 2 3 4 5 6 7 8 9 10 11 12 13 14 15 16 17 18 19 20 21 22 23 24 25 26 27 28 29 30 31 32 33 34 35 36 37 38 39 40 41 42 43 44 45 46 47
//SAMPLE    JOB
//STEP1     EXEC
//INCARD    DD
//OUTDISK   DD
//  XXXXXXXXXXXXX
//STEP2     EXEC
//INDISK    DD
//INTAPE    DD
//OUTTAPE   DD
//OUTPRINT  DD
```

Now you know about the format and structure of JCL. You have even coded a couple of parameters. You can tell a keyword parameter from a positional parameter. You are ready to learn some of the most basic parameters—the ones that you will use for almost every job. Chapter 2 will teach you how to code elementary jobs.

chapter two

Elementary JCL

In this chapter, we will take a closer look at the very basic building blocks of JCL—the JOB, EXEC, and DD statements. You will learn to define a job using these three types of statements along with a delimiter statement and a null statement.

Unit record sets have the fewest complications as far as DD statements are concerned. Therefore, in this chapter, you will learn to define these types of data sets. You will learn how to define tape and disk data sets in later chapters.

Most large-scale computer systems include as part of their software a special JCL procedure that causes the system to compile, link edit, and execute a source program. The programmer can then run this special procedure, treating it as a single-step job. In this chapter, you will be writing the JCL for one-step jobs; multiple-step jobs will be introduced in Chapter 4.

When you have completed this chapter you will be able to write

- An elementary JOB statement
- An elementary EXEC statement
- An elementary DD statement for a unit record data set
- A delimiter statement
- A null statement
- A one-step job using all of the above

The JOB Statement

1. The primary function of the JOB statement is to signal the beginning of a new job in the input stream. (It may also mark the end of the previous job.) It also gives the system some general information about the job. In this chapter, you will learn to write the JOB statements in the general format shown on the following page.

//jobname   JOB   [(accounting info)][,programmer-name][,CLASS=jobclass]

The brackets are used here to denote that the enclosed parameter is optional. There are other JOB statement parameters, but they either have default values or are used only in special situations. We need only the above parameters for the elementary statements in this chapter.

What entries are always required in a JOB statement?_____

- - - - - - - - - -

//; jobname; JOB

> The IBM system does not require you to include any JOB parameters. Your installation, however, will probably require you to use some, if not all, of the other parameters shown above. You will use all three as you work through this chapter.

2.   As you learned in Chapter 1, a jobname may be any word of up to eight characters. It may contain only the following characters.

A to Z

0 to 9

@ $

The first character may not be a number. Notice that a space is not a valid character for JCL names.

Which of the following are acceptable jobnames?

_____ (a) SORTRECS   _____ (d) JO'S JOB

_____ (b) 23900A   _____ (e) UPDT#1

_____ (c) EMPLUPDATE   _____ (f) $45

- - - - - - - - - -

a, e, and f (b starts with a digit; c is too long; d contains two illegal characters—apostrophe and space)

3.   Accounting information may contain any of the characters that jobname may contain. In addition, it may contain a hyphen. Installations usually use this parameter to bill the computer's time. Therefore, each installation usually creates its own department/project coding system. For the purposes of this book, we will charge our jobs to the Personnel Department, Unit 3, Training Group, Project 101. The code we will use will be PERS#3,TR-101.

Which of the following would be a correct JOB statement using only the "accounting info" parameter?

_____ (a) //SCORTEST JOB   PERS#3,TR-101

```
_____ (b) //SCORTEST  JOB    (PERS#3,TR-101)

_____ (c) //SCORTEST  JOB    ACCT=PERS#3,TR-101
```
- - - - - - - - - -

b

4.   The programmer's name is usually included to identify the output and so that the computer operator knows whom to call in case of problems or questions. It may contain any characters acceptable in a jobname, as well as periods. Names that include special characters, such as apostrophes and spaces, may also be coded, but they must be enclosed in single quotes. Since the apostrophe is normally a single quote also, IBM requires apostrophes enclosed in single quotes to be represented by two consecutive quotes, as shown below.

```
//UPDATE    JOB   (PERS#3,TR-101),'O''DONNEL')
```

Believe it or not, this will come out on the printout as O'DONNEL.
   Which of the following are correct?

_____ (a) JONES	_____ (d) L.J. PETERS, JR.
_____ (b) JOHN EDWARDS	_____ (e) M.R. KAUFMAN
_____ (c) MARY-SMITH	_____ (f) "O'BRIEN"

- - - - - - - - - -

a and e (b contains a space; c contains a hyphen; d contains a comma; f has single and double quotes reversed. b, c, and d would be correct if they were enclosed in single quotes.)

5.   Now let's look at the CLASS parameter. A sample classification scheme is shown in Table 1. The operating system schedules jobs according to their hardware requirements. Each installation usually defines various jobclasses (coded A through O) to describe different types of jobs. For example, CLASS=A may mean a job that runs for less than 1 minute; CLASS=L might mean any job that uses a great deal of printer output. Jobs of each class are grouped together into a waiting line, or *queue* (pronounced *kew*). When the system is ready to take a new job, it accesses the first one in the appropriate queue, according to what hardware is now available.
   The CLASS parameter, then, specifies what type of job you have, but your installation defines exactly what the different class indicators mean. As a relatively new programmer, you will probably be told what CLASS to use. If you omit the CLASS parameter, the system will define a default class. (Your installation determines what default class will be used.) Some installations have the system reject the job if it exceeds the limits of the jobclass.

Table 1

Here is an example of an installation with a specific hardware configuration.

     Maximum storage: 2M
     Tape units: 10
     Disk units: 10
     Printers: 2
     Terminals: 10

This installation might assign jobclasses as shown.

class	maximum run time	tape units	disk units	printer	terminal	max storage
A						64K
B	30 min.	none	0–2	yes	yes	96K
C						128K
D						160K
E						96K
F	45 min.	none	0–4	yes	yes	128K
G						160K
H	60 min.	none	3–6	yes	yes	128K
I						160K
J						96K
K	60 min.	1–2	0–2	yes	yes	128K
L						160K

M, N, and O are reserved for special applications that require more than six disk units, more than 60 minutes, or more than 160K. Special permission must be obtained from the system manager to exceed those limits.

Refer back to the JOB statement format in frame 1. Which of the following are correct codings for a class parameter?

_____ (a) ,CLASS=B

_____ (b) ,"CLASS=C"

———— (c) ,CLASS=D

———— (d) ,CLASS=jobclass

– – – – – – – – – –

a, c

6. Here are rules for coding a JOB statement using the parameters you have just studied.

- // must be in columns 1 and 2.

- Jobname must start in column 3.

- JOB must be preceded and followed by at least one space.

- Accounting information and programmer's name are positional parameters. If accounting information is omitted, a comma must still precede programmer's name to show that it is the second parameter. Example:

```
//NEWRUN    JOB   ,JARSENZ,CLASS=A
```

- If the programmer's name is omitted, and keyword parameters follow the accounting information, you may omit the comma for the programmer's name. (When the system encounters a keyword parameter, it can figure out that the final positional parameters have been omitted.) Example:

```
//NEXTRUN   JOB   (PERS#3,TR-101),CLASS=B
```

- If both positional parameters are omitted, their commas need not be coded. Examples:

```
//FIRSTRUN JOB
//LASTRUN   JOB   CLASS=T
```

- CLASS is a keyword parameter. If used, it must follow the positional parameters.

Which of the following JOB statements are correct?

(a) `// SORTRECS JOB   (PERS#3,TR-101),D.FELICIA`

(b) `//GROUPEMP JOB   C.J.JOHNSON,CLASS=N`

(c) `//LISTEMP   JOB   (PERS#3,TR-101),A.MILLS`

(d) `//CHECK#8   JOB   (PERS#3,TR-101),J.LEE,CLASS=D`

(e) `//COMPCOB   (PERS#3,TR-101),F.N.ABBOTT`

– – – – – – – – – –

c and d (In a, the jobname does not begin in column 3; in b, the accounting information is omitted but a comma does not precede the programmer's name; in e, the word JOB is omitted.)

7.   Now you are going to write a JOB statement. Assume that your name is CARTER, and that your accounting information is PERS#3,TR-101. Your job is named JOBONE, and should be run in jobclass E.

- - - - - - - - - -

```
//JOBONE   JOB   (PERS#3,TR-101),CARTER,CLASS=E
```

> Whenever you check your coding:
>
>   Make sure you used the correct spacing;
>   Make sure you used correct punctuation.

8.   Code the JOB statement for a job that updates an employee master data set. Create a valid jobname. Use the standard (for this guide) accounting information and your own name. Assign a jobclass of A.

- - - - - - - - - -

    Here is an example of a correct answer.

```
//UPDTEMP   JOB   (PERS#3,TR-101),R.A.ASHLEY,
//              CLASS=A
```

9.   It's time for plain old punctuation practice. Code each of the following as a JOB statement. Put each one on one line of the form below. (Review the rules in frame 6 before you begin.)

	jobname	accounting info	programmer's name	jobclass
(a)	CHECKDT	PERS#3,TR-101	yours	B
(b)	SUMYEAR	none	yours	C
(c)	FINDERRS	none	none	B
(d)	CORRERRS	PERS#3,TR-101	none	C
(e)	DROPACCT	none	none	default

| 1 | 2 | 3 | 4 | 5 | 6 | 7 | 8 | 9 | 10 | 11 | 12 | 13 | 14 | 15 | 16 | 17 | 18 | 19 | 20 | 21 | 22 | 23 | 24 | 25 | 26 | 27 | 28 | 29 | 30 | 31 | 32 | 33 | 34 | 35 | 36 | 37 | 38 | 39 | 40 | 41 | 42 | 43 | 44 | 45 | 46 | 47 |

(a) ├──┤

(b) ├──┤

(c) ├──┤

(d) ├──┤

(e) ├──┤

- - - - - - - - - -

```
//CHECKDT  JOB  (PERS#3,TR-101), your name, CLASS=B
//SUMYEAR  JOB  , your name, CLASS=C
//FINDERRS  JOB  CLASS=B
//CORRERRS  JOB  (PERS#3,TR-101), CLASS=C
//DROPACCT  JOB
```

The EXEC Statement

10.   Now let's consider the EXEC statement. Each job has at least one step. The EXEC statement tells the system the name of the program to be executed. Alternatively, it might refer to a *catalogued procedure*, which is a set of JCL statements that has been stored in one of the system's libraries. The general form of the EXEC statement is:

$$ //\text{[stepname]}\ \ \text{EXEC} \left\{ \begin{array}{l} \text{PGM=programname} \\ \text{[PROC=]procedurename} \end{array} \right\} $$

Items enclosed in brackets are optional. The stacked items within the braces mean that you must use one, but only one of the options. Neither brackets nor braces are coded.

   (a)   What parts of the EXEC statement are optional?_____

   _____

   (b)   The stepname has the same general format as a jobname. What

   characters can it contain? _____

- - - - - - - - - -

(a) Stepname; PROC=
(b) Letters (A to Z); numbers (0 to 9); $ @ #

11.   It's time now to consider system libraries. You can't execute a program or a procedure that the system can't find. Programs and procedures are often stored in various system and user libraries.

A library is a partitioned data set.

The system libraries are permanently mounted at most installations. That's one reason you can't use all the disk units at your installation; some of them are assigned to the libraries.

The Program Library contains programs. To be executed, a program must either be in the Program Library or included with your JCL. In the library, it is stored with a name, and you must use that name on your EXEC statement to get it.

If you code EXEC PGM=CUSTUPDT, the system will look in the Program Library for CUSTUPDT. If the system finds it, the program will be loaded and processing will begin. If not, you'll get a system message equivalent to "No such program," and the system will bypass your job and go about its business. (If your program is included with your JCL, or course, the system doesn't have to look for it.)

The Procedure Library contains sets of JCL statements that have been catalogued (which simply means that they have been placed in the Procedure Library). Like programs, each JCL procedure will have a name which you must use to access that procedure.

If you code EXEC SORTPROC, the system will look in the Procedure Library for SORTPROC and continue as above.

Answer the questions below in your own words.

(a)   At an IBM installation, what is a library?_____

_____

(b)   What type of library holds programs?_____

(c)   What type of library holds procedures?_____

(d)   If you specify EXEC PGM=CALCRANG, which library will the system look in?_____

(e)   If you specify EXEC PROC=LOADTAPE, which library will the system look in?_____

(f)   If you specify EXEC CARDPRIN, which library will the system look in?_____

(g)   What is a catalogued procedure?_____

_____

(h)   Suppose you submit a job that contains this statement:

```
//SORTSTEP EXEC STDSORT
```

You get back a system message that means "No such procedure, job bypassed." What could be wrong? _____

_____

- - - - - - - - - -

(a) A partitioned data set; a place where programs and JCL procedures are stored
(b) Program library
(c) Procedure library
(d) Program library
(e) Procedure library
(f) Procedure library
(g) A set of JCL statements that has been given a name and stored in the procedure library
(h) A lot of things could have gone wrong. Perhaps you thought of one or more of the following:

STDSORT could be a program, not a catalogued procedure; in that case you should have said PGM=STDSORT.

You could have been given the wrong code name for the procedure you need.

Someone may have erased STDSORT from the procedure library and you didn't know it.

The procedure library, for whatever reason, may not have been available at the time your program was run.

12. Here are two examples of EXEC statements that you can use as guides to practice writing your own.

Example 1: We want to execute a catalogued procedure that will compile, link, and go. The name of the procedure is COLINKGO. Either of the following statements will execute this procedure.

```
//TESTCODE EXEC COLINKGO
//TESTCODE EXEC PROC=COLINKGO
```

The procedure, in turn, will contain EXEC statements calling on the compiler program, the link editor, and the resultant load module. We have included the stepname, although it is optional.

Example 2: We want to execute an IBM utility program (a program furnished by IBM for general purposes) that will format and print out a data set from cards. The name of this program is IEBPTPCH. The EXEC statement would be:

```
//        EXEC PGM=IEBPTPCH
```

Here we have omitted the stepname to show you the format. Now you write statements for the following.

(a) You wish to execute a program called SUMACCTS. This step does not need a name, so don't use one.

(b) You wish to execute COLINKGO. Your installation requires stepnames on all EXEC statements. No fair copying ours.

- - - - - - - - - -

(a) //   EXEC PGM=SUMACCTS
(b) //RUNSTEP EXEC COLINKGO
    (Most programmers omit PROC=)

13.   Let's assume you are planning to run a one-step job to execute a program named LISTEMPS. Your installation requires you to use jobclass B, with names for each job and step. Write JOB and EXEC statements using your name and our standard accounting information.

- - - - - - - - - -

```
//MYJOB    JOB    (PERS#3,TR-101),ASHLEY,CLASS=B
//MYSTEP   EXEC   PGM=LISTEMPS
```

The DD Statement

14.   Now we'll consider the Data Definition (DD) statement. This statement tells the system where to find or put each data set the program requires. Each type of data set has its own parameters. In this chapter, you will learn to define input and output unit record data sets. The general format of a DD statement is shown below.

```
//ddname    DD    parameters
```

The ddname names the *statement*, not the data set. It is used to relate the DD statement to the file name used in the source program.

   The following example shows how the ddname appears in a COBOL program.

COBOL Program:
SELECT TRANSACTIONS ASSIGN TO UT-S-INCARDS

JCL:
//INCARDS DD etc.

(a) In what columns must // appear?_____

(b) In what column must the ddname begin?_____

(c) What does the ddname identify?_____

- - - - - - - - - -

(a) 1 and 2; (b) 3; (c) the DD statement

15. Each data set used in a jobstep must have a DD statement with a unique ddname (except in special cases when you combine or concatenate data sets). All of the DD statements for a step must follow the EXEC statement for that step, but the exact order of the separate DD statements is unimportant. Suppose you want to run a one-step job that uses two input unit record data sets (A and B), one printer file for normal output, and one printer file for error messages.

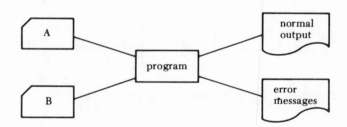

Which sequence of JCL statements below is correct?

(a) JOB
    DD (for A)
    DD (for B)
    EXEC
    DD (for normal output)
    DD (for error messages)

(b) JOB
    EXEC
    DD (for error messages)
    DD (for B)
    DD (for normal output)
    DD (for A)

(c) DD (for A)
    DD (for B)
    DD (for normal output)
    DD (for error messages)
    EXEC
    JOB

- - - - - - - - - -

b

16.   Most installations use the same input device for JCL statements and for unit record input data sets. Therefore, if you wish to use an input unit record data set, the data set must be placed on the same device as the JCL input stream. You must put it right in with your JCL statements. This is accomplished as follows:

   (1)   Code the DD statement:

       `//DDNAME     DD     *`

      The asterisk parameter (*) notifies the system that the input data set immediately follows the DD statement in the input stream.

   (2)   Put the data records immediately after that DD statement.

   (3)   Follow the data set with a statement with /* in columns 1 and 2.

When the system encounters the asterisk parameter, it spools all the records that follow the asterisk until it finds one that starts with // or /*. The spooled data is then used as the input data set. Some programmers like to follow every unit record data set with a delimiter statement—a statement that contains /* in columns 1 and 2—just for safety's sake.

   Unit record data sets in the input stream are called *instream* data sets. Here is a sample job.

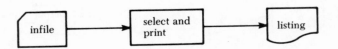

   (a)   Write the DD statement for the input data set.

   (b)   When you are preparing your JCL to run this job, where would you put the INFILE records? _____

   (c)   You must be careful that none of the data records begin with // or /*. Why?_____

- - - - - - - - - -

(a) `//INFILE     DD     *`
(b) Immediately following the DD statement
(c) Because either symbol signals the end of the data set (Subsequent records would not be treated as input records but as JCL statements, probably causing an abend.)

17.   Output unit record data sets do not require much in the way of a description. You must tell the system to send the output to a unit record

device; the system will do the rest. The format of the DD statement is shown below.

```
//ddname    DD    SYSOUT=value
```

The value you assign to the SYSOUT parameter depends heavily on the local installation. Each installation is free to come up with its own code system for types of unit record output. For our purposes in this book, we will always use SYSOUT=A, which we define as meaning a printer with regular paper and a 132-character line. (SYSOUT=B usually means a card punch.)

Here is the job from the previous frame.

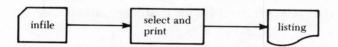

(a) Write the DD statement for the print data set.

(b) True or false? IBM defines SYSOUT=A to mean a 132-character printer with regular paper. _____

- - - - - - - - - -

(a) //LISTING   DD   SYSOUT=A
(b) false (Each installation defines its own.)
    Check your coding for item a above, looking specifically at spacings.

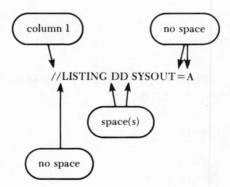

The Null Statement

18.   Most programmers mark the end of a job with a null statement. This is a statement that has // in columns 1 and 2 and no other information.

(a) What type of statement marks the end of a job?_____

(b) Code a statement to mark the end of a job._____

- - - - - - - - - -

(a) null; (b) //

The Complete One-Step Job

19. The job below contains one step. It executes a program called CHANLIST, which prints out a list of new customers and a separate list of terminated customers from a file of customer change records.

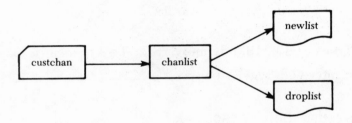

Here is the sample coding.

```
//LISTCHAN JOB  (PERS#3,TR-101),FERNANDEZ, CLASS=A
//ONLYSTEP EXEC PGM=CHANLIST
//CUSTCHAN DD    *
    (input records go here)
/*
//NEWLIST  DD    SYSOUT=A
//DROPLIST DD    SYSOUT=A
//
```

The program diagrammed below uses as input two unit record data sets and puts out a combined listing of all the names. Code a job to execute this program. Use jobclass B, and create jobname and stepname as needed. Be sure to indicate where input records will be inserted.

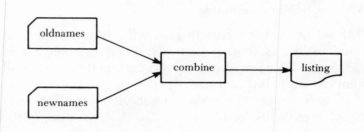

```
- - - - - - - - - -
//NEWJOB    JOB  (PERS#3,TR-101),R.ASHLEY, CLASS=B
//NEWSTEP   EXEC PGM=COMBINE
//OLDNAMES DD    *
    (records for this data set)
/*
//NEWNAMES DD    *
    (records for this data set)
/*
//LISTING   DD    SYSOUT=A
//
```

Be sure to check your coding for:

Correct placement in columns
No embedded spaces in parameters
Correct placement of data sets
Valid jobname, stepname

Any format or syntax errors in JCL will cause your job to be bypassed by the system. If your CLASS parameter is spelled CALSS, or you have put spaces around the equal sign, you will get a system message, but no run.

This Self-Teaching Guide cannot give you the detailed, perfectionist examination of your coding that the system will. But careful comparison of your coded statements with our sample coding can give you feedback to approximate that examination. As you check each of your answers against ours, play the role of the computer. Be nasty. Remember: the computer shows no mercy.

Summary Exercise

This job contains one step. It executes a program called SELPRINT, which selects and prints the names and phone numbers of college graduates from a unit record data set of job applicants. Use the ddnames shown in the system flow diagram, but create your own jobname and stepname. Use a jobclass of B. Indicate where your input data set will be placed.

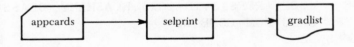

- - - - - - - - - -

```
//YOURJOB  JOB  (PERS#3,TR-101),YOURNAME, CLASS=B
//YOURSTEP EXEC PGM=SELPRINT
//APPCARDS DD    *
    (your input records go here)
/*
//GRADLIST DD     SYSOUT=A
//
```

In Chapter 2, you have learned how to code elementary JOB, EXEC, and DD statements. You can code a one-step job, invoking either a program or a catalogued procedure. You have learned how to enter a data set in the input stream and how to send output to a printer. You have learned seven parameters (accounting info, programmer's name, CLASS=, PGM=, PROC=, *, and SYSOUT=). You are well on your way to being able to control the operating system through the use of JCL.

chapter three

Data Sets on Tape

So far you have written complete jobs using basic JOB, EXEC, and DD statements. You have used DD statements for input unit record data sets, as well as for print output. In this chapter you will expand your use of DD statements to include definitions of data sets on tape. This task involves six new DD parameters, many with subparameters, to handle both input and output tape data sets. You will continue to work with simple systems that require only one-step jobs while you develop skills in describing the tape data sets.

When you complete your study of this chapter, you will be able to

- Write a parameter to tell the system what type of hardware is needed for a tape data set (UNIT)

- Write a parameter to describe records and blocks in a data set (DCB)

- Write a parameter to tell the system what to do with a data set after the jobstep (DISP)

- Write a parameter to indicate what type of label is needed (LABEL)

- Write a parameter to specify a name for a data set (DSN)

- Write a parameter to tell the system which reel of tape contains the data set (VOL)

- Code a complete job including DD statements for unit record, print, and tape data sets

- Code complete DD statements for input and output tape data sets

Characteristics of Tape Data Sets

1.   Records in unit record data sets must have a fixed length and may not be blocked or grouped in any way. Tape data sets, however, are different.

- Records on a tape data set may be fixed or variable in length; the records can be kept as long as necessary.

- Records on a tape data set may be blocked (or grouped) to save space and I/O time.

- A tape reel may contain several small data sets, or a large data set may require more than one tape reel.

- An installation will have a number of separate tape drives, maybe several different types.

- Tape may be used for either input or output data sets.

- Each tape data set may contain label records in addition to data records.

The DD statement for a tape file must give enough information about the data set so the system can locate an input one or create the required output one.

Refer to the information above as necessary and determine which of the features below you might expect to find in a DD statement for a tape data set.

_____ (a) whether the tape reel is used for input or output

_____ (b) a SYSOUT parameter

_____ (c) which tape drive holds the reel

_____ (d) how many records are in a block

_____ (e) an * parameter

_____ (f) the length of records in the data set

– – – – – – – – – –

a, c, d, and f (Remember that SYSOUT is a unit record parameter, while * refers specifically to instream data.)

2.   When a tape data set is used, the DD statement must give much more information than for an instream or print data set. The usual parameters used to describe tape data sets are listed below.

DCB	gives record and block information
DSN	gives the data set name
DISP	specifies whether the data set is input or output, and tells the system what to do with it after the job
UNIT	specifies the type of hardware unit needed for the data set
VOLUME	tells exactly which tape reel is needed

LABEL   tells the system what labels to look for or write

The UNIT, VOLUME, LABEL, and DCB parameters are very dependent on each other. UNIT specifies the actual hardware (tape drive), VOLUME specifies exactly which tape reel, LABEL indicates how to find the data set on the reel (or how to label it), and DCB tells how the records are arranged within the tape reel. When a tape is created, the DCB and DSN are usually written into the label. When the tape is read, the system can check the DSN, then get DCB information from the label.

    (a)   Which of the six parameters listed above would you expect to specify for an input file that already exists on a labeled tape reel? _____

    (b)   Which would you expect to specify for an output tape data set that will have a complete label? _____

_____

    (c)   Which of these size records would be applicable to a tape data set—80 bytes, 133 bytes, 16 bytes, or 5000 bytes? _____

_____

- - - - - - - - - -

(a) DSN, DISP, UNIT, VOLUME, and LABEL
(b) DCB, DISP, DSN, UNIT, VOLUME, and LABEL (all of them)
(c) all would be appropriate for a tape data set

The DISP Parameter

3. The DISP (disposition) parameter specifies whether the data set already exists or will be created in this jobstep. DISP also tells the system what to do with the data set after this jobstep. In addition, DISP can specify what to do with the data set if the step abends. We'll learn to handle that later. The simple format for the DISP parameter is as follows.

DISP=(status, disposition)

The status subparameter tells whether the data set already exists or will be created by the jobstep.

OLD indicates the data set already exists.

NEW indicates the data set will be created.

Other values (SHR and MOD) will be treated later.

The disposition subparameter tells the system what to do with the data set after the jobstep.

KEEP means the system should save the data set.

DELETE means the system may reuse the tape for another data set.

Several other values can be specified. Some of them will be treated later.

A DISP parameter of (NEW,KEEP) specifies that the data set is to be created in this jobstep, which means that it is to be used for output, and the system should keep it. Another job or jobstep will probably be using the data set later.

(a)   Is the DISP parameter positional or keyword?_____

(b)   Are the subparameters positional or keyword?_____

(c)   Match the following.

   _____ (A) first subparameter   (1) disposition
   _____ (B) second subparameter   (2) status
                                      (3) NEW or OLD
                                      (4) KEEP or DELETE
                                      (5) tells whether the data set
                                          exists or will be created
                                      (6) tells what to do with the
                                          data set after the jobstep

(d)   What does a DISP specification of (NEW,DELETE) tell you

      about the use of a data set in the jobstep?_____

      _____

      What about its use after the jobstep?_____

- - - - - - - - - -

(a) keyword; (b) positional; (c) A—2,3,5; B—1,4,6; (d) use is output; no use afterwards

4.   The one-step job diagrammed below shows a program in which one tape data set is used as input and another for output. In this job an update program produces a new master file using the old master file and change records that specify the updates. A report of the changes is printed out at the end.

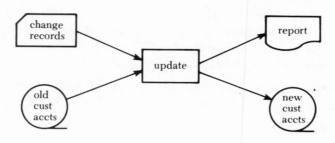

After the jobstep, the OLD CUST ACCTS data set should be deleted. The NEW CUST ACCTS data set should be saved for the next round of updates. The DD statements for the two tape data sets would include DISP parameters as shown below.

```
//OLDCUST  DD   DISP=(OLD,DELETE)
//NEWCUST  DD   DISP=(NEW,KEEP)
```

The in-stream and print files do not require DISP parameters.

(a)   Code a DISP parameter for an input tape data set that should be kept after the jobstep._____

(b)   Code a DISP parameter for a tape data set to be created in this step that should be kept after the jobstep._____

(c)   Code the DISP parameter for an input tape data set that should be deleted after the jobstep._____

(d)   Suppose you are going to run a one-step job. In that job you are going to create a data set, then use it in processing, but you don't ever want to use it after the jobstep is finished. Code a DISP parameter for this data set._____

- - - - - - - - - -

(a) DISP=(OLD,KEEP)
(b) DISP=(NEW,KEEP)
(c) DISP=(OLD,DELETE)
(d) DISP=(NEW,DELETE)

Again a reminder to check your coding carefully. Make sure that
There are no embedded spaces
Parentheses are in place
Commas separate subparameters
Spelling is perfect

5.   If a DISP parameter is not specified for a tape data set, the system assumes (NEW,DELETE)—the default value for DISP. If your data set is created in the step and may be deleted, you can safely omit the DISP parameter. If your data set is created in the step and you want to keep it, you can specify DISP=(,KEEP). The system will assume the missing status is NEW. You must include the comma when you omit the first subparameter, since these are positional subparameters. The system will not understand if you use incorrect format. For example:

DISP=(KEEP) would be read by the system as status=KEEP; since the status must be NEW or OLD, your JCL would be rejected.

DISP=,KEEP could not even be interpreted, since the system expects a parenthesis and NEW or OLD after the equal sign. Again your JCL would be rejected.

If you omit the second disposition subparameter, the system will assume that the data set should have the same disposition at the end of the jobstep as it had before it. Hence, if you code only a first subparameter of NEW, or omit a first subparameter, the system will assume DELETE. If you code only a status of OLD, the system will assume KEEP. Thus DISP=OLD means (OLD,KEEP); the data set existed before the job and will exist after it. The parentheses are not necessary when only the first subparameter is coded.

Match the following.

_____ (a) (NEW, DELETE)   (1) NEW
_____ (b) (OLD,KEEP)   (2) (,DELETE)
                                   (3) (,KEEP)
_____ (c) (NEW,KEEP)   (4) OLD
_____ (d) (OLD,DELETE)   (5) omit the DISP parameter
                                   (6) none of these

- - - - - - - - - -

(a) 1, 2, 5; (b) 4; (c) 3; (d) 6

6. Specify whether each of the following describes a new or an old data set, and whether or not the data set will exist after the jobstep is completed.

   (a) DISP=(,KEEP)_____

   (b) DISP=(,DELETE)_____

   (c) DISP=OLD_____

   (d) DISP=NEW_____

   (e) no DISP parameter for the tape_____

- - - - - - - - - -

(a) new, will exist; (b) new, will not exist; (c) old, will exist; (d) new, will not exist; (e) new, will not exist

The UNIT Parameter

7. The UNIT parameter tells the system how many of what kind of hardware units are needed for the data set. The format is shown below.

$$\text{UNIT} = (\begin{Bmatrix} \text{device type} \\ \text{group name} \end{Bmatrix}[, \begin{Bmatrix} \text{unit count} \\ \text{P} \end{Bmatrix}])$$

The first subparameter tells the system what kind of I/O device should be assigned.

- Device type is used to specify the exact type of device, such as 2400.

- Group name is used when the installation has all the same type of tape device or the programmer doesn't care which one is used. The installation creates the group name, but the most commonly used name is TAPE.

The second subparameter is optional. It tells the system how many of the specified unit types you want.

- Unit count is the actual number of units—2, 3, or whatever.

- P means "one unit for each volume"; this is coded only if your volumes are all needed simultaneously. It is considered greedy or "piggy" by other programmers.

- The subparameter is optional because the default is 1; you get one tape drive per tape data set if you don't request otherwise.

Examples: UNIT=(TAPE,2) requests any two tape units; UNIT=2400 requests one 2400 tape drive unit.

(a)   Is the UNIT parameter positional or keyword?

_____

(b)   Are the subparameters positional or keyword?

_____

(c)   Code a UNIT parameter to request one tape unit of any type.

_____

(d)   Code a UNIT parameter to request one 2400 tape unit for each

volume in the data set._____

- - - - - - - - - -

(a) keyword; (b) positional; (c) UNIT=TAPE or UNIT=(TAPE,1) (Recall that parentheses may be omitted if only one subparameter is used.) (d) UNIT=(2400,P)

The DCB Parameter

8.   The DCB parameter of a DD statement gives information about the Data Control Block. This is a record placed in storage when a data set is opened that tells the system how to read or write the file. It is concerned with such factors as record length, block length, format of records, buffering, etc. Most of the Data Control Block is picked up from the header label of an old data set. For a new data set on tape, however, you will have to specify DCB information to create the label.

In this Self-Teaching Guide, we will be concerned with three major DCB subparameters. They are listed at the top of page 45.

LRECL (logical record length)

RECFM (record format)

BLKSIZE (block or physical record length)

These subparameters are all keyword, and so may be in any order within the DCB. If more than one is used, all must be enclosed in parentheses and separated by commas. In this book we will use only two record format codes: F for fixed-length records and FB for fixed-length, blocked records.

The record format shown below is fixed-length, blocked (FB). The record length is 100 bytes, and the block length is 300 bytes. The DCB parameter is DCB=(BLKSIZE=300,LRECL=100,RECFM=FB).

	BLOCK 1				BLOCK 2
gap — between blocks	Record 1	Record 2	Record 3		Record 1
	100 bytes	100 bytes	100 bytes		100 bytes

(a)   Code the DCB parameter for this format.

BLOCK	
Record 1	Record 2
550 bytes	550 bytes

(b)   Code the DCB parameter for this format.

BLOCK
Record
3300 Bytes

- - - - - - - - - -

(a) DCB=(BLKSIZE=1100,LRECL=550,RECFM=FB)

(b) DCB=(BLKSIZE=3300,LRECL=3300,RECFM=F)

Reminder: The subparameters of DCB can be in any sequence, but they must be separated by commas and enclosed in parentheses.

9.   Assume you are going to use an output data set on tape, which should be kept after the jobstep. It will require only one of any type of tape unit. The

records will be 500 bytes long, with a blocking factor of 10 (10 records per block). Code a DD statement using the ddname OUTTAPE and three DD parameters for tape files. Use the correct method for continuing your statement on a second line.

– – – – – – – – – –

```
//OUTTAPE  DD   DISP=(NEW,KEEP),UNIT=TAPE,
//              DCB=(LRECL=500,RECFM=FB,BLKSIZE=5000)
```

The VOL Parameter

10.   VOL is short for VOLUME. The VOL parameter identifies the actual volume or tape reel on which the data set is stored, or will be stored if it is a NEW data set. The format follows.

```
VOL=([PRIVATE],[RETAIN],[volume-sequence-number],
       [volume-count],[SER=(serial number, . . . )])
```

A great deal of information can be specified in the VOL parameter, but the usual format is VOL=SER=serial number. The descriptions below cover all the above options, however.

-   PRIVATE, RETAIN, volume-sequence-number, and volume-count are positional subparameters; if any is used, the commas for all must be represented. If none are used, however, no commas are needed before SER.

-   PRIVATE means the tape reel can't be used for any other purpose while it is mounted, unless another program specifically requests that volume. The reel is dismounted at the end of the step unless RETAIN is coded.

-   RETAIN means don't dismount the private volume; it will be needed later in the job.

-   Volume-sequence-number tells which volume in the data set you want to begin with. The operator will automatically begin with the first reel, unless you specify a number larger than 1.

-   Volume-count tells the maximum number of volumes you will need for an output data set.

-   SER=(serial number, . . .) gives the serial number on the header label for as many volumes as are included. Up to six characters may be used for the serial number.

Refer to the information above and determine the meaning of the following VOL parameter.

```
VOL=( ,RETAIN, , ,SER=19T149)
```

(a)   How many volumes are in this data set?_____

(b)   Which volume will the jobstep begin with?_____

(c)   Can the data set be used by other jobs?_____

(d)   What will happen to the tape reel after the jobstep?

_____

(e)   What is the exact number of the tape reel?_____

(f)   Why are there three commas in a row?_____

_____

- - - - - - - - - -

(a) 1 (volume-count is omitted); (b) 1 (volume-sequence-number is omitted); (c) no (tape volumes are always PRIVATE); (d) it will not be dismounted (RETAIN is coded); (e) 19T149 (the SERial number); (f) volume-sequence-number and volume-count are omitted

11.   The VOL parameter gives much information. Suppose, for example, you have an input data set on three tape reels; all three volumes are private and should be dismounted at the end of the jobstep. The serial numbers of the volumes are 24T921, 24T922, and 24T923. The VOL parameter for this data set is

```
VOL=(PRIVATE, , , ,SER=(24T921,24T922,24T923))
```

Whenever you have no information about which volume or how many there are, assume the default of 1. Notice in the example above:

The RETAIN subparameter is omitted;

Volume-sequence-number is omitted;

Volume-count is omitted (this is input, not output).

Remember, if only the SER subparameter is used, all the positional commas may be omitted. This is the usual way the VOL parameter is coded. For practice, however, we will ask you to code some VOL parameters using the various subparameters available to you.

(a)   Write a VOL parameter for an output tape data set on private volumes that should be retained. The maximum number of volumes is 4. Use serial numbers 24T100, 24T101, 24T102, and 24T103.

(b) Write a VOL parameter for an input tape data set that is public, has only one reel, and whose serial number is 24T301.

(c) Write a VOL parameter for an input tape data set on two volumes. It is private but should be left on the tape drive after the jobstep. The serial numbers are 24T616 and 24T621.

(d) Write a VOL parameter for an output tape data set that is public and has a maximum of five volumes.

- - - - - - - - - -

(a) VOL=(PRIVATE,RETAIN,,4,SER=(24T100,24T101,24T102, 24T103))
(b) VOL=SER=24T301
(c) VOL=(PRIVATE,RETAIN,,,SER=(24T616,24T621)) Note that you don't code the volume count, since this is an input data set.
(d) VOL=(,,,5)

The LABEL Parameter

12.   The LABEL parameter gives the system information about what to put on the label it creates (for an output data set), or what to look for on the label of an input data set. The information given tells the system how to process the data set. The format is:

LABEL=([data-set-sequence-number],[label-type],[file-protection],

$$\left[\begin{Bmatrix} IN \\ OUT \end{Bmatrix}\right], \left[\begin{Bmatrix} EXPDT=yyddd \\ RETPD=nnnn \end{Bmatrix}\right])$$

All of the subparameters above are optional; in fact, the LABEL parameter is often not needed at all. But when it is used, commas must replace any missing positional subparameters. The exception occurs when only the last subparameter (the keyword one) is used. Then the commas may be omitted, just as with VOL=SER.

- Data-set-sequence-number is coded if an input data set is not the first one on a reel (volume).

- Label-type tells the system what type of label should be looked for or created. There are many different types, but we shall stick to SL, for standard labels, which is the default.

- File-protection gives information to secure an output data set.

PASSWORD means that in order for the file to be used for either input or output, the operator must key in a password (assigned by the system).

NOPWREAD means that a password is not needed to read the data set, but one is needed to write on the data set.

No entry means that no password is needed for reading or writing on the data set.

- IN,OUT is never used for tapes, so we will always use a comma for this subparameter.

- The last subparameter, the only keyword subparameter, has two possibilities, both of which indicate how long the new data set should be kept on the tape. The expiration date is placed in the label of each data set.

EXPDT = yyddd specifies the expiration data for the data set. The data set cannot be deleted until after the date given. For example, EXPDT = 89222 means the set will be kept until the 222nd day of 1989.

RETPD = nnnn specifies the number of days that the data set should be retained—its retention period. The system will convert this into an expiration date.

Refer to the explanations above to interpret the following LABEL parameter.

`LABEL=( ,SL,PASSWORD, ,RETPD=0030)`

(a) When can this data set be deleted?_____

(b) Does this data set require a password?_____

(c) What is the meaning of the SL subparameter?_____

_____

- - - - - - - - - -

(a) after 30 days; (b) yes; (c) standard labels

13.   The LABEL parameter below indicates an output data set that has standard labels, requires a password for writing only but may be read without one, and will expire on the first day of 1989.

`LABEL=( ,SL,NOPWREAD, ,EXPDT=89001)`

Now write LABEL parameters for the data sets described below.

(a)   An output tape data set has standard labels, requires no password, and should be kept until the last day of 1987.

_____

(b)   An output data set has standard labels, requires a password for any operation, and should be retained for 90 days.

_____

(c)   An input data set is third on its reel._____

- - - - - - - - - -

(a) LABEL=(,,,,EXPDT=87365) or LABEL=EXPDT=87365
(b) LABEL=(,SL,PASSWORD,,RETPD=0090)
(Notice that SL may be included or omitted in either case.)
(c) LABEL=3

The DSN Parameter

14.   Every data set must have a Data Set Name. The system generates DSNs for unit record data sets. You must create names for data sets on tape. The DSN is stored on the data set label and is used by the system to identify the data set. It is not the same as the ddname, which identifies the DD statement.

Why so many names? Suppose you have a tape file of data that is used by ten different applications. Each application program may call the tape by a different name, which usually refers to the way the data set is used in that application. The ddname is the name by which the program refers to the data set.

The DSName, however, is constant. This name is created when the data set is created, and it is placed on the label. Thus, any future use of the data set must identify it by this DSName so that the system can identify the correct data set. The DD statement for the data set will include the ddname, to connect the data set to whatever it is called in the program, and the DSN parameter, to connect the desired data set to the name on the header label.

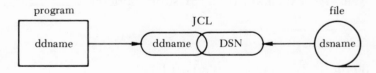

The format of the DSN parameter is shown below.

DSN=dsname or DSNAME=dsname

For existing files, you will be given the DSName. This is essential in order to know what to code. For new files you create, you will assign the DSName according to rules at your installation. The general IBM rules are that it use the standard JCL character set and, if it is more than eight characters long, it must have a period at least every eight characters. A maximum of 44 characters, including periods, is permitted. Many installations have added to these rules to create consistent data set names for their applications.

(a) Which name is used in JCL to link the application program to the DD statement?_____

(b) Which name is used to link the JCL DD statement to a specific header label?_____

(c) Different names are represented by ddname and DSName. What does DD stand for?_____

What does DS stand for?_____

(d) In an actual tape data set, where would you find the DSName?

_____

(e) //INTAPE DD DISP=OLD,UNIT=TAPE,DSN=TNG58AR6

What is the name of this statement?_____

What is the name on the header label of the data set?

_____

- - - - - - - - - - - -

(a) ddname; (b) DSName; (c) data definition, data set; (d) in the header label; (e) INTAPE, TNG58AR6

15. In the DD statement, the DSN parameter must be included for every tape file, whether new or old. For new data sets, the DSName is included in the label. For old data sets, the DSName is used to find the appropriate data set.

(a) For which type of data sets would you need to specify a DSN parameter: input tape, output tape, input unit record, print?

_____

(b) Does the programmer create a DSName for an old or for a new tape file?_____

(c) Write a DSN parameter for a data set that includes CUST0503 on its label._____

- - - - - - - - - - -

(a) input tape and output tape; (b) new; (c) DSN=CUST0503

Defining Input Tape Data Sets

16. When you define an input tape data set, the data set and its label already exist. You have studied six new parameters in this chapter that may be used to describe tape files. Some of these are needed and some are not when the tape data set is used for input.

DCB Not needed. This information is on the label.

DISP Needed. For input, DISP must specify OLD (or SHR, as you'll learn later) for status. The other subparameter may be KEEP or DELETE as needed.

DSN Needed. The system uses this to locate the data set.

UNIT Needed. You must always request a tape drive for your volume.

VOL Needed. At least SER must be specified. Add the positional parameters if you need them.

LABEL Not needed unless you need one or more of its subparameters. The system will assume standard labels and the first position on the reel unless you specify otherwise.

Assume you have an input data set to use in order processing. The ddname is ORDERS. The DSName on the label is SAL532XC. The serial number of the volume is 24T619. At the end of the jobstep, this file is to be kept. Its DD statement would look like this.

```
//ORDERS    DD   DISP=OLD,UNIT=TAPE,VOL=SER=24T619,
//               DSN=SAL532XC
```

Notice that the DISP parameter could have specified (OLD,KEEP) and the VOL positional subparameters could have been included.

The following exercises specify the ddname for each tape data set inside the tape symbol. Other information you will need is indicated. Write complete DD statements for these input tape data sets.

(a) At the end of the jobstep the data set is kept. The labels are standard.

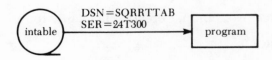

(b)   At the end of the jobstep the data set is deleted. This data set is the first one on the reel.

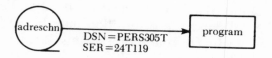

- - - - - - - - - -

(a) `//INTABLE    DD    DISP=OLD,UNIT=TAPE,DSN=SQRRTTABB,`
    `//                 VOL=SER=24T300`
(b) `//ADRESCHN  DD    DISP=(OLD,DELETE),UNIT=TAPE,`
    `//                 DSN=PERS305T,VOL=SER=24T119`

17.   Code a job to run a program called LISTREPT in jobclass F, as shown below. Use the same accounting information as in previous chapters. The tape will be used again for other jobs. (Refer to frame 16 for the list of parameters.)

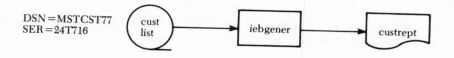

- - - - - - - - - -

```
//jobname   JOB   (PERS#3,TR-101),yourname,CLASS=F
//stepname  EXEC  PGM=LISTREPT
//CUSTLIST  DD    DSN=MSTCST77,UNIT=TAPE
//                DISP=(OLD,KEEP),VOL=SER=24T716
//CUSTREPT  DD    SYSOUT=A
//
```

Defining New Tape Data Sets

18.   A new tape data set does not exist before you create it. Therefore, you must give the system all the information it needs to create the data set and labels. The parameters available for use are shown below.

   DCB   Needed. The blocksize, record length, and record format are very important. They must be put into the label by the system, and there are no standard values for tape data sets.

If you specify these values in your source program also, that will override your JCL.

DISP   Optional if the data set is to be deleted. The status is always NEW, and the disposition may be KEEP or DELETE according to your requirements. If you want both defaults (NEW,DELETE), DISP may be omitted.

DSN   Needed. You must tell the system what name to put on the data set label.

LABEL   Needed only if you wish to specify one or more of its positional subparameters or an expiration date. Standard labels and one data set per reel are assumed if you omit this parameter.

UNIT   Needed. Always.

VOL   Needed only if you want to use a specific tape reel or one of the other VOL subparameters.

Assume you are creating an output tape data set to use in updating an inventory. The ddname will be INVENTRY. The DSName on the label is to be INV78CY. This data set is to be kept for use in other programs for the next year. You do not wish to assign the data set to a specific reel. You do want the records, which are 98 bytes long, to be blocked by 50. This file's DD statement would look like this.

```
//INVENTRY DD   DSN=INV78CY,DISP=(NEW,KEEP),UNIT=TAPE,
//               DCB=(BLKSIZE=4900,LRECL=98,RECFM=FB),
//               LABEL=RETPD=0365
```

Notice that the DISP subparameter NEW could have been omitted. Now write complete DD statements for the new tape data sets described below.

(a)   The data set to be created will contain records each 75 bytes long, blocked by 10. It is to be used later by another program and needs a specific retention period of 30 days. The data set name on the standard label is to be TAPE1492. Any available tape reel may be used.

(b)   This data set will contain blocks of 8 records, each 200 bytes long. It will be used in several other programs over the next year, at the end of which time it can be deleted. The system should put the data set on tape reel PP7321. The data set name is to be HX32TOPS.

- - - - - - - - - -

```
(a) //TPSTEP2     DD   DSN=TAPE1492,DISP=(NEW,KEEP),
    //                 UNIT=TAPE,DCB=(BLKSIZE=750,
    //                 LRECL=75,RECFM=FB),LABEL=RETPD=0030
(b) //TPSTEP3     DD   DSN=HX32TOPS,DISP=(,KEEP),
    //                 UNIT=TAPE,DCB=(BLKSIZE=1600,
    //                 LRECL=200,RECFM=FB), VOL=SER=PP7321,
    //                 LABEL=RETPD=0365
```

Notice that these parameters are all keyword; they can be coded in any
sequence.

19.   Code a job to run the following program, using jobclass D. The output
data set is to have the data set name TAPE17B. The records are 80 bytes long
and are to be blocked by 10 on the tape. The tape label is to indicate a
retention period of 180 days. You don't care exactly what tape reel it resides
on. Create a jobname and stepname as you wish, but use the indicated
ddnames.

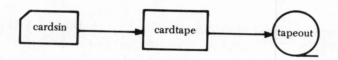

- - - - - - - - - -

```
//EXERCIZE  JOB   (PERS#3,TR-101),RYL,CLASS=D
//THESTEP   EXEC  PGM=CARDTAPE
//CARDSIN   DD    *
       data set goes here
/*
//TAPEOUT   DD    DSN=TAPE17B,UNIT=TAPE,
//                DISP=(NEW,KEEP),DCB=(BLKSIZE=800,
//                LRECL=80,RECFM=FB),LABEL=RETPD=0180
//
```

Summary Chart

DD Parameter Summary for Data Sets in One-Step Jobs

	unit record (input)	*print*	*tape (old)*	*tape (new)*
DCB	——	optional[1]	optional	required
DISP	——	——	required	required[2]
DSN	——	——	required	required
LABEL	——	——	optional	optional
SYSOUT	——	required	——	——
UNIT	——	——	required	required
VOL	——	——	required	optional
*	required	——	——	——

[1]You might use DCB=BLKSIZE=linelength if you use a nonstandard length line. Some installations require DCB=BLKSIZE=133 for every print data set.
[2]Optional if DISP=(NEW,DELETE).

Summary Exercise

Code the complete update job shown below. Use jobname TAPESUMM, stepname STEPTAPE, jobclass E, and program LOOKSTAR. Use ddnames as specified inside the symbols. All needed information is given in the chart.

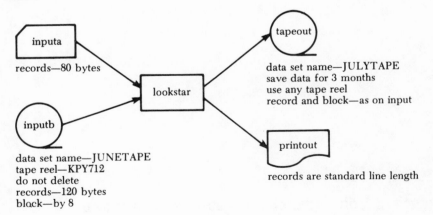

inputa

records—80 bytes

lookstar

tapeout

data set name—JULYTAPE
save data for 3 months
use any tape reel
record and block—as on input

inputb

data set name—JUNETAPE
tape reel—KPY712
do not delete
records—120 bytes
block—by 8

printout

records are standard line length

Answer to Summary Exercise

```
//TAPESUMM JOB  (PERS#3,TR-101),PAUL,CLASS=E
//STEPTAPE EXEC PGM=LOOKSTAR
//INPUTA   DD   *
     put input data set here
/*
//INPUTB   DD   DSN=JUNETAPE,UNIT=TAPE,
//              DISP=(OLD,KEEP),VOL=SER=KPY712
//TAPEOUT  DD   DSN=JULYTAPE,UNIT=TAPE,
//              DISP=(NEW,KEEP),LABEL=RETPD=0090,
//              DCB=(BLKSIZE=960,LRECL=120,RECFM=FB)
//PRINTOUT DD   SYSOUT=A
//
```

VARIATIONS

1. DD parameters may be coded in any order.
2. In INPUTB, you could have used DISP=OLD.
3. In TAPEOUT, you could have used DISP=(,KEEP).
4. DD statements may be coded in any order.

chapter four

Multi-Step JCL

Inherent in the whole concept of JCL is the idea of being able to piece together several existing programs to make up a job. As we discussed in the first chapter, a job may have several jobsteps. You have learned how to code a single step. In this chapter, you will learn how to code a job with more than one jobstep.

In the process, you will learn some more parameters and subparameters. You will also learn how to pass a data set from one jobstep to a later jobstep in the same job.

When you have completed this chapter you will be able to

- Code a REGION parameter in a JOB or EXEC statement
- Code a TIME parameter in a JOB or EXEC statement
- Code a DD statement for a tape data set that is to be passed to a later step in the same job
- Code a DD statement for a tape data set that is to be received from a previous step in the same job
- Code a DD statement for a temporary tape data set
- Code a conditional disposition for a data set
- Code a complete multi-step job involving unit record and tape data sets, including temporary and passed data sets

Review of Jobs, Jobsteps, and Statements

1. The job represented at the top of page 59 includes three steps.

    Step 1   Transaction cards are the input data. They are sorted into ascending sequence by customer number and placed on the output transaction tape in the new sequence.

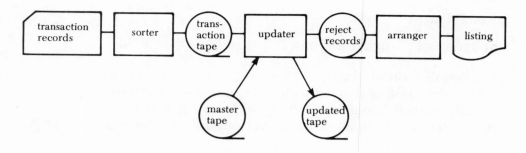

Step 2   A master tape is updated, using the output of step 1 as the transaction file. The result is an updated master tape and an output tape of transaction records that were rejected for any of a number of reasons.

Step 3   In the third step, the reject records are rearranged according to the coded reason for rejection. They are printed out in groups, one for each reason.

Review what you learned in Chapter 1 as you answer these questions.

(a)   How many JOB statements would you need to run this job?_____

(b)   How many EXEC statements would you need to run this job?

_____

(c)   How many DD statements would you need for each step?_____

_____

– – – – – – – – – –

(a) one
(b) three
(c) Step 1—two (transaction cards and transaction tape)
     Step 2—four (transaction tape, master tape, updated tape, and reject records tape)
     Step 3—two (reject records tape and listing)

The REGION Parameter

2.   When you write the JCL for a job, you can specify the amount of memory space your program will need. Or you can use the default amount for your installation. The REGION parameter can be specified in either the JOB statement or the EXEC statements. REGION is a keyword parameter that specifies an even number of kilobytes of storage needed for the job or step to execute. (If you do specify an odd number, the system will allocate the next higher even number.) The format follows.

REGION=regionsizeK

Examples:

```
REGION=8K    REGION=192K
```

For the job illustrated in frame 1, you might need a maximum of 64K. Write a complete JOB statement, using the positional parameters you have already learned. Assign the job to jobclass F. Remember that keyword parameters may be in any sequence but must follow positional parameters.

```
//UPDATING JOB  (PERS#3,TR-101),ASHLEY,CLASS=F,
//              REGION=64K
```

or

```
//UPDATING JOB  (PERS#3,TR-101),ASHLEY,REGION=64K,
//              CLASS=F
```

3. Region size may vary greatly for the different steps in a job. The job in frame 1, for example, might need 8K for step 1, 64K for step 2, and 12K for step 3. In this case, you might not use the REGION parameter in the JOB statement, but include it in each EXEC statement instead. This will allow the system to release storage space for other jobs being run at the same time when you don't need it. (Other users, and the operator, will appreciate your courtesy.) For example, the first EXEC statement might read as follows.

```
//SORTSTEP EXEC PGM=SORTING,REGION=8K
```

Write EXEC statements for the other two steps, specifying the REGION parameter. Remember that the PGM= parameter is positional, even though it looks like a keyword parameter.

```
//UPDATES  EXEC PGM=UPDATES,REGION=64K
//ARRANGES EXEC PGM=ARRANGES,REGION=12K
```

(As before, you may have used different stepnames.)

The TIME Parameter

4. Each computer installation has a default time limit for each job, in addition to a default region size. The programmer can, however, override the default time by specifying a TIME parameter in either the JOB or EXEC statement, or both.

The effect of the TIME parameter is to specify the maximum CPU time allowed for the job. If the job then exceeds the CPU time, the system interrupts the run, terminates the job (or the step), prints out a system message, and goes on about its business. You can use this feature to avoid programs getting into closed loops, extended waits for other programs to release time, and so on. It is extremely important to specify a short time such as 2 minutes when testing the logic of a new program with small amounts of data. The format for the TIME parameter is as follows.

TIME=(minutes,seconds)

Examples:

TIME=18   TIME=(1,30)   TIME=(,15)

Notice that, while TIME is a keyword parameter, its subparameters are positional.

Write TIME parameters for the following expected CPU times.

(a)   30 seconds_____

(b)   30 minutes_____

(c)   three quarters of a minute_____

(d)   three quarters of an hour_____

(e)   seven and a half minutes_____

- - - - - - - - - - -

(a) TIME=(,30)   (b) TIME=30   (c) TIME=(,45)   (d) TIME=45
(e) TIME=(7,30)

(Many programmers add a "fudge factor" of 10% or so.)

5.   In general, you would specify TIME in either the JOB statement or the EXEC statements. Like region size, time needed is generally estimated for the first run and adjusted in line with system messages. Compilers often require as much as 192K, but compile time may be less than one minute.

When a region size is specified in a JOB statement, the size is equal to that needed for the largest step. The same region may be used over again by the system. When you specify REGION in EXEC statements instead, you state what you need for each step. However, when you specify a TIME parameter in a JOB statement, you must specify the *sum* of the times for all steps in the JOB. If you specify TIME on the JOB and EXEC statements, all the time limits are observed by the system. For example, if you specify TIME=(4,30) on the JOB statement and TIME=2 on each EXEC statement, each step will be terminated if it exceeds two minutes, and the entire job will be terminated if it exceeds four and a half minutes.

Assume that the maximum time expected to run the steps of your three-step job (frame 1) are 1 minute for the first step, 3 minutes for the second, and 30 seconds for the third. Complete the statements below to allow the necessary time.

```
(a)  //UPDATING JOB   (PERS#3,TR-101),name,TIME=_____
(b)  //SORTSTEP EXEC PGM=SORTING,TIME=_____
(c)  //UPDATES   EXEC PGM=UPDATES,TIME=_____
(d)  //ARRANGES EXEC PGM=ARRANGES,TIME=_____
```

- - - - - - - - - -

(a) TIME=(4,30) (b) TIME=1 (c) TIME=3 (d) TIME=(,30)

6.   The job diagrammed below requires 12K bytes for the programs. The first step needs a maximum of 3 minutes while the next step needs only 30 seconds of CPU time. The jobclass is D. Create job and stepnames as you write the following statements.

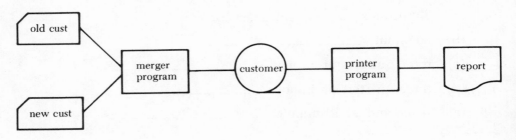

    (a)   JOB statement

    (b)   EXEC statement for the first step

    (c)   EXEC statement for the second step

- - - - - - - - - -

```
(a) //PREPARE  JOB  (PERS#3,TR-101),name,REGION=12K,
    //               CLASS=D
(b) //MERGESTP EXEC PGM=MERGER,TIME=3
(c) //PRINTSTP EXEC PGM=PRINTER,TIME=(,30)
```

7.   Suppose that you wish to run COMPLKGO (a compile, link, and go procedure). It needs 128K and always takes the program time plus 4 minutes

to compile and link. (This time, the program will take 3 minutes.) Write an EXEC statement for such a jobstep. Specify all the parameters.

- - - - - - - - - -

```
//MERGER    EXEC COMPLKGO,TIME=7,REGION=128K
```

Passing Data Sets from One Step to Another

8. Most multi-step jobs involve using the same data set in more than one step. For example:

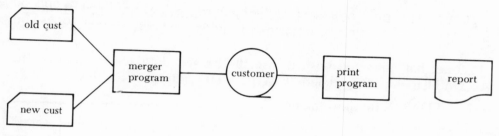

In this job, you want to create the tape data set in the first step, then use it in the next. If the two steps were two separate jobs, you would use DISP=(NEW,KEEP) in the first job and DISP=(OLD,KEEP) in the second job.

Another disposition value, PASS, is used in multi-step jobs when a data set is to be reused within the same job.

$$DISP=(\left\{{NEW \atop OLD}\right\},\left\{{KEEP \atop DELETE \atop PASS}\right\})$$

For this job, in the first step you would specify DISP=(NEW,PASS). In the second step you specify DISP=(OLD,KEEP).

Refer back to the job diagrammed in frame 1. At the end of the job you will retain only the updated tape and the listing. Write DISP parameters for the data sets in these steps.

	data set	*step name*	
(a)	TRANTAPE	(SORTSTEP)	_____
(b)	TRANTAPE	(UPDATES)	_____
(c)	REJTAPE	(UPDATES)	_____
(d)	UPDATEDT	(UPDATES)	_____

- - - - - - - - - -

(a) DISP=(NEW,PASS) or DISP=(,PASS)
(b) DISP=(OLD,DELETE)
(c) DISP=(NEW,PASS) or DISP=(,PASS)
(d) DISP=(NEW,KEEP) or DISP=(,KEEP)

9.   Whenever data sets are reused within a job, use PASS as a DISP subparameter. This ensures that the operator won't dismount your tape, or the system release your tape unit for another job. When you do pass a data set, your subsequent DD statements for that data set are greatly simplified. You only need specify the "three D's"—ddname, DSName, and DISP.

The DD statement below describes an output data set to be created in the SORTER step of a job, and passed to a later step.

```
//SORTOUT   DD   DSN=FILET1,DCB=(BLKSIZE=800,LRECL=80,
//               RECFM=FB),UNIT=TAPE,DISP=(NEW,PASS)
```

Assume that now you wish to use the passed data set as input to the UPDATER step, then delete it. Write a DD statement for this later step.

(Use UPDATIN for the ddname.) _____

- - - - - - - - - -

```
//UPDATIN   DD   DSN=FILET1,DISP=(OLD,DELETE)
```

10.   When a data set is reused within a job, you can write DSNames in one of three ways.

DSN=dsname	A standard dsname.
DSN=*.ddname	Refers back to an earlier DD statement. The system will get the DSName from that statement.
DSN=*.stepname.ddname	Refers back to a DD statement in an earlier step.

For example, the job below uses the same tape in two steps.

DSN=TPMST23

```
//UPDATER  EXEC  ...
//TAPEIN   DD    ...
//TAPEOUT  DD    ...DSN=TPMST23
    .
    .
    .
//REPORTER EXEC  ...
//INTAPE   DD    ...DSN=*.UPDATER.TAPEOUT...
                 (refers back to earlier step)
```

Look again at the DD statement you wrote in frame 9. Write an alternative DSN parameter for this data set._____

- - - - - - - - - -

DSN=*.SORTER.SORTOUT

> One advantage to using refer-backs in DSNames is to keep JCL easy to maintain. Then if a DSName is changed, you have to make only one change—the only time the DSName is spelled out. Refer-backs may also be used with the DCB parameter. You may refer back to any DD statement in the same job that contains the correct DCB information.

Temporary Data Sets

11.   Often you may want to create a data set for use only within a job. That is, the data set does not exist before the job begins and will not exist after the job is over. Sometimes temporary data sets are used in one-step jobs, but usually they are found in multi-step jobs. A few special rules apply to the DD parameters for temporary data sets.

DISP | The first DD statement for a temporary data set in a job must specify status NEW. The last DD statement for a temporary data set in a job should specify disposition DELETE. (If it doesn't, the temporary data set will be deleted anyway.) The disposition of a temporary data set may be PASS or DELETE, but never KEEP.

DCB | Must be included when the data set is NEW. You can refer back to other DD statements.

DSN | Optional when DISP=NEW. If omitted, the system makes up a DSN for the data set. If you omit the DSN and then reuse the temporary data set, you must use the DSN refer-back (*.stepname.ddname). If you use DSN, the name should begin with two ampersands. Example: &&TEMPY

VOL | Never specify VOL for temporary data sets. Let the system choose a scratch volume.

(a) Write a DISP parameter for a temporary data set in a one-step job. _____

(b) Consider a three-step job. A temporary tape data set is created in the first step (PRESTEP) and passed to the next. The records are 100 bytes long, blocked by 4. Write a DD statement for DDTEMP1 for the first step. Let the system assign the DSN.

(c) The same data set is used in the second step (PROCSTEP), then passed on to the third. Write a DD statement for DDTEMP2.

(d) In the last step (PRINSTEP) the temporary data set is used for the last time. Write its DD statement (DDTEMP3).

```
(a) DISP=(NEW,DELETE)
(b) //DDTEMP1   DD    UNIT=TAPE,DCB=(RECFM=FB,
    //                LRECL=100,BLKSIZE=400),DISP=(NEW,
    //                PASS)
(c) //DDTEMP2   DD    DSN=*.PRESTEP.DDTEMP1,DISP=(OLD,
    //                PASS)
(d) //DDTEMP3   DD    DSN=*.PRESTEP.DDTEMP1,DISP=(OLD,
    //                DELETE)
```

12. Which of the following could be valid DD statements for temporary data sets?

```
(a) //STEPONE   DD    DSN=&&TEMPY,UNIT=TAPE,
    //                DISP=(OLD,KEEP)
(b) //STEPONE   DD    UNIT=TAPE,DISP=(NEW,DELETE),
    //                DCB=(BLKSIZE=600,LRECL=100,
    //                RECFM=FB)
(c) //STEPTWO   DD    UNIT=TAPE,DISP=(NEW,PASS)
(d) //STEPTWO   DD    DSN=&&TEMPY,DISP=(OLD,DELETE)
```

----

b and d (In a, you cannot KEEP a temporary data set; in c, no DCB information is included.)

13. Assume you are writing a two-step job. In the first step (STEPA) you will be creating a temporary data set on tape named &&SORTED, with blocks containing ten 58-byte fixed-length records. In the next step (STEPB) you will use the same data set to print out a report. Then the data set may be deleted.

    (a)   Write the two DD statements for &&SORTED. Create your own ddnames.

    (b)   Write the two DD statements without using the temporary data set name. Use a DSN refer back in your second DD. Create your own ddnames.

- - - - - - - - - -

```
(a) //STEPAT1  DD   DSN=&&SORTED,UNIT=TAPE,DISP=(NEW,
    //               PASS),DCB=(RECFM=FB,LRECL=58,
    //               BLKSIZE=580)
    //STEPBT1  DD   DSN=&&SORTED,DISP=(OLD,DELETE)
(b) //STEPAT1  DD   UNIT=TAPE,DISP=(NEW,PASS),
    //               DCB=(RECFM=FB,LRECL=58,BLKSIZE=580)
    //STEPBT2  DD   DSN=*.STEPA.STEPAT1,DISP=(OLD,
    //               DELETE)
```

Conditional Disposition

14. As we have seen, the disposition subparameter of DISP (KEEP, PASS, or DELETE) specifies what the system should do with the data set if the jobstep terminates normally. However, if the jobstep terminates abnormally (abends), you may have different instructions for the system. For example, in an update step, you may wish to handle the data sets as follows.

Data set	Status	Normal end	System or user abend
old master	old	delete	keep
transactions	old	delete	keep
new master	new	keep	delete

A third subparameter of DISP allows you to specify conditional disposition—what to do if the step abends. The format is shown below.

$$DISP=(\begin{Bmatrix} NEW \\ OLD \end{Bmatrix}, \begin{Bmatrix} KEEP \\ DELETE \\ PASS \end{Bmatrix}, \begin{Bmatrix} KEEP \\ DELETE \end{Bmatrix})$$

Example:

`DISP=(NEW,PASS,KEEP)`

This DISP parameter specifies that the data set is new, to be created in this step. If the step finishes normally, the data set is to be passed to the next step. If not, the data set is to be kept. (An extra job may be run later to determine the cause of the abend.)

    (a)   Write a DISP parameter for a transactions file following the chart on p. 67. _____

    (b)   Write a DISP parameter for a new master file following the chart on p. 67. _____

- - - - - - - - - -

(a) `DISP=(OLD,DELETE,KEEP)`
(b) `DISP=(NEW,KEEP,DELETE)`

15.   The system flow diagram below represents a two-step job under normal conditions. Consider the two data sets produced in the first step. (The ddnames are shown.)

    If the first step abends, TRANS and ERRORS are to be kept, since the user can print them with another program to determine the cause of the abend. Write complete DISP parameters for both data sets for the first step.

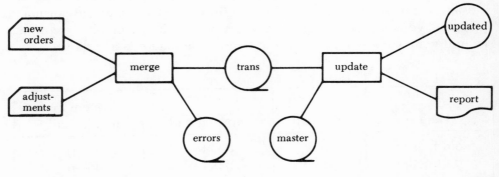

    (a)   TRANS_____

    (b)   ERRORS_____

- - - - - - - - - -

(a) `DISP=(NEW,PASS,KEEP)`
(b) `DISP=(NEW,KEEP,KEEP)`

16. The chart below summarizes the possible combinations you have learned for the DISP subparameters.

Status	Normal disposition	Conditional disposition
NEW	DELETE	DELETE
		KEEP
	PASS	DELETE
		KEEP
	KEEP	DELETE
		KEEP
OLD	DELETE	DELETE
		KEEP
	PASS	DELETE
		KEEP
	KEEP	DELETE
		KEEP

Remember extra commas if you omit the first or second subparameter and use a later one.

What happens if you omit the conditional disposition? When an abend occurs before a data set is allocated, the conditional disposition defaults back to the status of the data set before the step was run. However, if the data set *has* been allocated at the time of the abend, then the default is to the normal disposition. It is safest to always code your conditional disposition for permanent data sets.

- You may omit DISP if DISP=(NEW,DELETE,DELETE).

- If DSN parameter is omitted, you should code PASS or DELETE for the normal disposition (because it must be a temporary data set). PASS is the default disposition for temporary data sets.

- Data sets that didn't exist before the job won't exist afterward unless you so specify. New data sets are DELETEd if the job abends unless you specify KEEP.

- Data sets that did exist before the job still exist afterward unless you DELETE them. OLD sets are KEPT if the job abends unless you specify DELETE.

Refer back to the system flow diagram in frame 15. Assume that, in case of normal termination, the old master is to be deleted while the updated master is to be kept. In case of abend, the reverse is true. Write DISP parameters using no defaults.

MASTER_____

UPDATED_____

- - - - - - - - - -

```
DISP=(OLD,DELETE,KEEP)
DISP=(NEW,KEEP,DELETE)
```

17. The diagram below represents a two-step job.

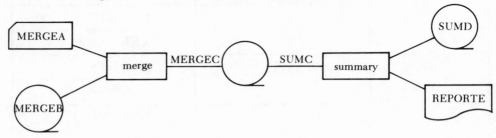

Step 1. MERGSTEP
         Use program MERGE, 1 minute, 12K storage.
         MERGEA
         Input unit records; enter in job stream.
         MERGEB
         Input tape, serial number 8731. DSName MAJTAPE; delete if normal ending, otherwise keep.
         MERGEC
         Output tape. Use a temporary DSName; pass if normal ending, otherwise delete. Records are 120 bytes, blocked by 20.

Step 2. SUMSTEP
         Use program SUMMARY, 1 minute, 12K storage.
         SUMC
         Input tape; delete when finished whether normal or not.
         SUMD
         Output tape. Use same blocking as SUMC; keep whatever is on the tape, no matter how the program ends; assign your own DSName.
         REPORTE
         Output print.

Write a complete job named MONTHEND. Show where data set A
would be inserted in the job stream.

```
//MONTHEND JOB  (PERS#3,TR-101),yourname,REGION=12K
//MERGSTEP EXEC PGM=MERGE,TIME=1
//MERGEA   DD    *
input records go here
/*
//MERGEB   DD   DSN=MAJTAPE,DISP=(OLD,DELETE,KEEP),
//              VOL=SER=8731,UNIT=TAPE
//MERGEC   DD   DCB=(RECFM=FB,LRECL=120,BLKSIZE=2400),
//              DISP=(,PASS),DSN=&&TEMP,UNIT=TAPE
//SUMSTEP  EXEC PGM=SUMMARY,TIME=1
//SUMC     DD   DISP=(OLD,DELETE,DELETE),DSN=&&TEMP
//SUMD     DD   DCB=*.MERGESTP.MERGEC,DSN=OUTAP1,
//              UNIT=TAPE,DISP=(,KEEP,KEEP)
//REPORTE  DD   SYSOUT=A
//
```

Summary Exercise

You are going to write a complete job. Specifications for all the data sets are given below.

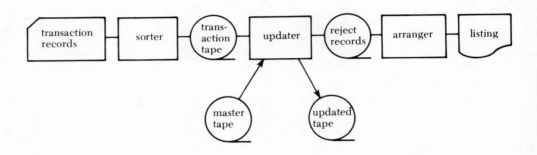

SORTSTEP	Use program SORTER, 1 minute, 10K storage.
INTRANS	Instream data set.
TRANOUT	Output tape. Record size is 67, blocked by 10. Create a temporary DSName.
UPSTEP	Use program UPDATER, 4 minutes, 40K storage.
TRANIN	Input tape. Delete when step is over.
MASTERTP	Input tape, number 9199, DSName is MASTER; keep this tape.
REJECTTP	Output tape. Same DCB information as TRANOUT; assign an appropriate DSName; delete this data set if the step abends.
UPDATETP	Output tape. Same DCB information as TRANOUT; keep data set no matter what happens; assign an appropriate DSName.
ARRASTEP	Use program ARRANGER, 1/2 minute, 6K storage.
REJECTIN	Input tape. Passed from previous step; delete in any case.
LISTING	Output print data set.

Now code the job. Specify the time and space requirements on the JOB statement.

Answer to Summary Exercise

```
//FOURJOB   JOB   (PERS#3,TR-101),yourname,TIME=(5,30),
//              REGION=40K
//SORTSTEP EXEC PGM=SORTER,TIME=1,REGION=10K
//INTRANS   DD    *
input data records go here
/*
//TRANOUT   DD    DSN=&&TRANTP,DCB=(RECFM=FB,LRECL=67,
//              BLKSIZE=670),UNIT=TAPE,DISP=(NEW,PASS)
//UPSTEP    EXEC PGM=UPDATER,TIME=4,REGION=40K
//TRANIN    DD    DSN=*.SORTSTEP.TRANOUT,DISP=(OLD,
//              DELETE)
//MASTERTP DD     DSN=MASTER,VOL=SER=9199,DISP=(OLD,
//              KEEP,KEEP),UNIT=TAPE
//REJECTTP DD     DSN=&&REJECT,DCB=*.SORTSTEP.TRANOUT,
//              DISP=(NEW,PASS,DELETE),UNIT=TAPE
//UPDATETP DD     DSN=UPMASTER,DCB=*.SORTSTEP.TRANOUT,
//              UNIT=TAPE,DISP=(NEW,KEEP,KEEP)
//ARRASTEP EXEC PGM=ARRANGER,TIME=(,30),REGION=6K
//REJECTIN DD     DSN=&&REJECT,DISP=(OLD,DELETE)
//LISTING   DD    SYSOUT=A
//
```

chapter five

Disk Data Sets

Data sets on disk have many of the same characteristics as those on tape. In this chapter we will be talking about sequentially organized disk data sets; handling direct and indexed disks is beyond the scope of this book. You will, however, have an excellent basis for learning about these more complex data set organizations through IBM JCL manuals or other reference books when you have finished studying this Self-Teaching Guide.

This chapter reviews and expands many DD parameters you learned earlier. The requirements and options for disk data sets are continually compared to those you have already been using in defining tape data sets.

When you complete this chapter, you will be able to

- Write a DD statement describing an input data set on disk

- Write a DD statement describing an output data set on disk

- Write a SPACE parameter to allocate space on a disk in terms of blocksize and number of blocks expected

- Differentiate between JCL requirements and options for disk and tape data sets

1. In concept, a disk volume is equivalent to a reel of tape. The data set can take up less than a volume, it can take up exactly one volume, or it can take up more than one volume. Every disk volume will have a unique serial number.

A tape volume may have a standard label, a label that isn't standard, or no label at all. However, every disk data set *must have a standard label.*

Like tape, when you use a disk data set, you must tell the system where to find it (old), or how to create it and where to put it (new). You do all this in your DD statement.

You would use each of the following parameters to describe a new tape file. Examine each one and indicate whether it would be needed to describe a new disk file.

_____ (a) The DCB parameter tells the system the size of the logical records and how to block them.

_____ (b) The DISPosition parameter tells the system whether the data set is NEW or OLD, what to do with it if the jobstep ends normally, and what to do with it if the jobstep abends.

_____ (c) The DSName parameter tells the system the name that you want placed on the data set's label.

_____ (d) The LABEL parameter tells the system whether to use standard labels and what to put in them (passwords, expiration dates, and so on).

_____ (e) The UNIT parameter tells the system how many of what type of I/O units should be made available for the data set.

- - - - - - - - - -

a, b, c, and e; d (LABEL) is needed only if you want to specify passwords, expiration dates, and so on.

2. You would use each of the following parameters to describe an input tape file. Examine each one and indicate whether it would be necessary to describe an input disk file.

_____ (a) The DISP parameter tells the system whether the data set is NEW or OLD, what to do with it if the jobstep ends normally, and what to do with it if the jobstep abends.

_____ (b) The DSName parameter tells the system the name that is stored on the data set's label. The system checks this to be sure it has actually located the correct data set.

_____ (c) The UNIT parameter tells the system how many of what type of I/O units should be made available for the data set.

_____ (d) The VOLUME parameter tells the system the serial number of the volume on which the data set can be found.

- - - - - - - - - -

all would be necessary

Review of DCB

3. Recall the format of the DCB parameter, and read the following disk-related statements.

Format 1:

DCB=(BLKSIZE=blocksize,LRECL=recordlength,RECFM=format)

Format 2:

DCB=*ddname   or   DCB=*.stepname.ddname

- You *must* specify DCB information for a new tape or disk data set. However, it is very dangerous to specify it for an existing data set because you will override the information on the label, and you may cause the data set to be read incorrectly.

- DCB for disk is just like DCB for tape.

- If no other data set in your job uses the same DCB information, use format 1. If a preceding DD statement in your job has the same DCB information, then use format 2; the system will copy the information from that DD statement.

- Specify blocksize and recordlength in bytes; for a fixed-length, blocked format, specify RECFM=FB.

Write the DCB parameters for each of the following output disk data sets.

(a)   This one-step job updates a customer account file. The output file should have 240-byte records, blocked by 20. Fill in the DCB parameter for NEWCUST.

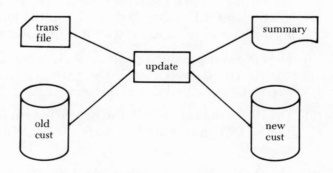

```
//NEWCUST   DD   _____
```

(b)   The job diagrammed at the top of page 77 creates two output files. Both have 122-character records, blocked by 100. Write the DCB parameters for each data set.

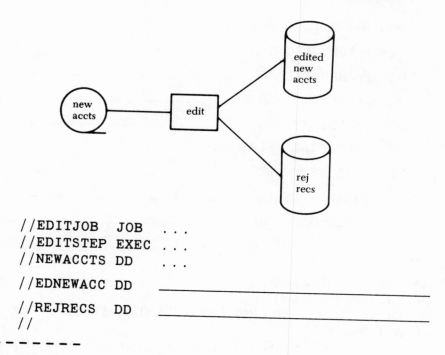

```
//EDITJOB   JOB   . . .
//EDITSTEP  EXEC  . . .
//NEWACCTS  DD    . . .

//EDNEWACC  DD    _____

//REJRECS   DD    _____
//
```

- - - - - - - - - -

```
(a) //NEWCUST   DD    DCB=(BLKSIZE=4800,LRECL=240,
    //                RECFM=FB)
(b) //EDNEWACC  DD    DCB=(BLKSIZE=12200,LRECL=122,
    //                RECFM=FB)
    //REJRECS   DD    DCB=*.EDNEWACC
```

4.   The two-step job diagrammed below creates a combined accounts file from a checking account file and a savings account file. Step 1 produces a temporary file in which the two input files have been merged and sorted in alphabetical order. Step 2 combines the accounts of customers who have both a checking and a savings account. All the disk files have records of 230 bytes. They are blocked by 100. Write all necessary DCB statements. If the parameter is not necessary write NO.

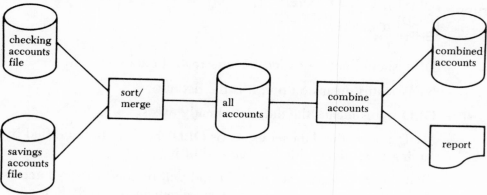

```
        //COMFILE   JOB   ...
        //SORTMERG  EXEC  ...
(a)     //CHECKFIL  DD    _____
(b)     //SAVFILE   DD    _____
(c)     //ALLTEMP   DD    _____
        //COMBINE   EXEC  ...
(d)     //ALLTEMP   DD    _____
(e)     //COMBACCT  DD    _____
(f)     //REPORT    DD    _____
        //
```

(a) NO (input data set)
(b) NO (input data set)
(c) DCB=(RECFM=FB,LRECL=230,BLKSIZE=23000)
(d) NO (input)
(e) DCB=*.SORTMERG.ALLTEMP (use your own stepname)
(f) NO

The DISP Parameter

5. Let's review the DISP parameter and look at a couple of new sub-parameters.
Format:

DISP=(status,normal-disposition,conditional-disposition)

Specific format:

$$DISP=(\begin{Bmatrix}NEW\\OLD\\MOD\\SHR\end{Bmatrix},\begin{Bmatrix}KEEP\\PASS\\DELETE\end{Bmatrix},\begin{Bmatrix}KEEP\\DELETE\end{Bmatrix})$$

- DISP should not be coded for unit record data sets.

- NEW status means output; it is the default.

- OLD status means the data set already exists.

- MOD means the data set exists (is OLD) but will be modified by having more data added to the end of it.

- SHR means the data set is OLD and will be used for read access only, so other users may use it simultaneously (in SHR mode);

use SHR whenever possible for input files; use OLD only when you need exclusive control of a volume.

– Normal-disposition tells what to do when the step ends normally. KEEP means "save this data set."
DELETE means "mark it for re-use"; the system may have it dismounted or may immediately assign the space for output by another job.
PASS means "this file will be used as input in a later step in this job; do not delete it, but do not dismount it either."
If the status is NEW, the default normal disposition is DELETE.
If the status is OLD, the default normal disposition is KEEP.

– Conditional-disposition tells what to do if the step abends.

Write the DISP parameters for each of the following data sets. Use defaults wherever possible. (All these examples are carried over from previous frames.)

(a) In this one-step job, OLDCUST should be deleted after NEWCUST is created. Therefore, it should not be used by other jobs simultaneously. NEWCUST, of course, should be kept after the step. But, if the step abends, NEWCUST probably contains invalid data. It should be eliminated and OLDCUST should be kept so the job can be run again after the problem is found.

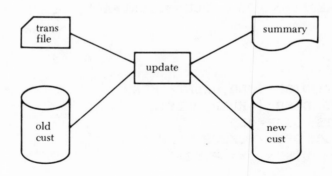

```
//UPDTJOB  JOB   . . .
//UPDTSTEP EXEC  . . .
//TRANSFIL DD    . . .

//OLDCUST  DD    _____
//SUMMARY  DD    . . .
//NEWCUST  DD    DCB=(BLKSIZE=4800,LRECL=240,

//               RECFM=FB),_____
//
```

(b) In the job diagrammed below, all data sets should be kept if the job ends successfully. If not, then NEWACCTS and REJRECS should be kept, but EDNEWACC (edited new accts) should be eliminated.

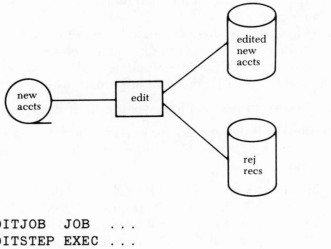

```
//EDITJOB   JOB   ...
//EDITSTEP  EXEC  ...

//NEWACCTS  DD    _____
//EDNEWACC  DD    DCB=(BLKSIZE=12200,LRECL=122,

//                RECFM=FB),_____

//REJRECS   DD    DCB=*.EDNEWACC,_____

//
```

- - - - - - - - - -

(a) OLDCUST: DISP=(OLD,DELETE,KEEP)
    NEWCUST: DISP=(,KEEP,DELETE)
(b) NEWACCTS: DISP=OLD
    EDNEWACC: DISP=(,KEEP,DELETE)
    REJRECS: DISP=(,KEEP,KEEP)

6. In this job, all files should be kept in all cases except ALLTEMP (all accounts), which should be deleted at the end of the job, whether normal or abnormal. Maintain exclusive control of ALLTEMP. If the DISP parameter is not necessary, write NO.

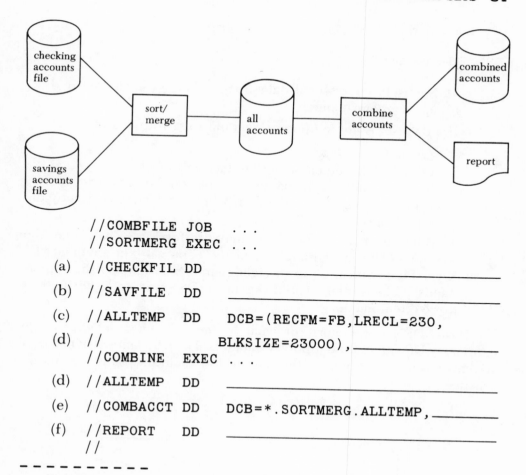

```
            //COMBFILE  JOB   ...
            //SORTMERG  EXEC  ...
  (a)   //CHECKFIL  DD     _____
  (b)   //SAVFILE   DD     _____
  (c)   //ALLTEMP   DD     DCB=(RECFM=FB,LRECL=230,
  (d)   //                     BLKSIZE=23000),_____
            //COMBINE   EXEC  ...
  (d)   //ALLTEMP   DD     _____
  (e)   //COMBACCT  DD     DCB=*.SORTMERG.ALLTEMP,_____
  (f)   //REPORT    DD     _____
            //
```

- - - - - - - - - -

(a) DISP=SHR
(b) DISP=SHR
(c) DISP=(,PASS)
(d) DISP=(OLD,DELETE,DELETE)
(e) DISP=(,KEEP,KEEP)
(f) NO (print file)

Review of DSName

7.   Recall these important things about the DSName parameter. All are true for disk as well as tape data sets.
   Format 1:

DSN=data-set-name

   Format 2:

DSN=*.ddname or DSN=*.stepname.ddname

Format 3:

DSN=&&tempname

- DSN must be coded for all data sets on volumes (that is, tape or disk) except temporary ones.
- If a data set is *not* temporary, you must use format 1 or 2.

    Format 1:
    Old . . . tells the name on the data set's label.
    New . . . dictates the name to be put on the data set's label.
    Format 2 should be used only if you are referring to exactly the same data set.
- If a data set is temporary, you may use format 3. "&&" cues the system, "this is a temporary data set." You can put anything you want for tempname (up to eight characters excluding the ampersands). The system will make up a DSName and substitute it for &&tempname.

Write DSN parameters for each of the following data sets. Use temporary DSNames for temporary data sets. The DSNames assigned by a systems analyst are shown on the system flow diagram. (This is common practice.)

(a)

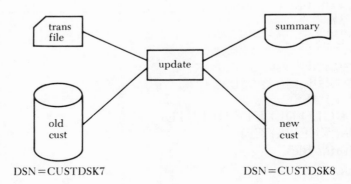

DSN=CUSTDSK7   DSN=CUSTDSK8

```
//UPJOB     JOB  . . .
//UPSTEP    EXEC . . .
//TRANSFIL  DD   . . .
//OLDCUST   DD   DISP=(OLD,DELETE,KEEP),_____
//SUMMARY   DD   . . .
//NEWCUST   DD   DCB=(RECFM=FB,LRECL=240,
//               BLKSIZE=4800),DISP=(,KEEP,
//               DELETE),_____
//
```

(b)

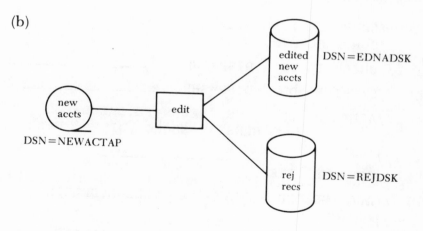

```
//EDITJOB  JOB  ...
//EDITSTEP EXEC ...

//NEWACCTS DD    DISP=OLD,_____
//EDNEWACC DD    DCB=(BLKSIZE=12200,LRECL=122,
//               RECFM=FB),DISP=(,KEEP,DELETE),
//               _____
//REJRECS  DD    DCB=*.EDNEWACC,DISP=(,KEEP,
//               KEEP),_____
```

- - - - - - - - - -

(a) OLDCUST: DSN=CUSTDSK7
     NEWCUST: DSN=CUSTDSK8
(b) NEWACCTS: DSN=NEWACTAP
     EDNEWACC: DSN=EDNADSK
     REJRECS: DSN=REJDSK

8. Code the DSN parameters for this job.

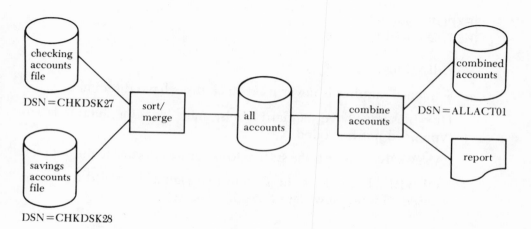

```
        //COMBFILE JOB   ...
        //SORTMERG EXEC  ...
(a)     //CHECKFIL DD    DISP=SHR,_____
(b)     //SAVFILE  DD    DISP=SHR,_____
(c)     //ALLTEMP  DD    DCB=(RECFM=FB,LRECL=230,
        //               BLKSIZE=23000),DISP=(,PASS),
        //               _____
        //COMBINE  EXEC  ...
(d)     //ALLTEMP  DD    DISP=(OLD,DELETE,DELETE),
        //               _____
(e)     //COMBACCT DD    DCB=*.SORTMERG.ALLTEMP,
        //               DISP=(,KEEP,KEEP),_____
        //REPORT   DD    ...
        //
```

(a) DSN=CHKDSK27
(b) DSN=SAVDSK27
(c) DSN=&&TEMPFIL
(d) DSN=&&TEMPFIL or DSN=*.SORTMERG.ALLTEMP
(e) DSN=ALLACT01

Review of LABEL

9. Recall the format of the LABEL parameter, and read these disk-related statements.
    Format:

$$LABEL=(sequence\text{-}number, label\text{-}type, \begin{Bmatrix} PASSWORD \\ NOPWREAD \end{Bmatrix}, \begin{Bmatrix} IN \\ OUT \end{Bmatrix},$$

$$\begin{Bmatrix} EXPDT=yyddd \\ RETPD=nnnn \end{Bmatrix})$$

For disk files:

- Sequence-number is never used since disks have direct access.

- Disk files must have standard labels; since this is the default, label-type need not be coded.

- PASSWORD requests the system to assign a password to the data set.

- NOPWREAD requests the system to assign a password that must be used to write new data onto the data set.

- IN means the disk data set can be used for input only.

- OUT means the disk data set can be used for output only. (IN and OUT are used with Fortran programs.)

- EXPDT means to put an expiration date on the label; 89057 means the 57th day of 1989; the system will refuse to DELETE the data set before that day.

- RETPD means to save the data set so-many days; 100 means 100 days after creation. The system calculates and stores the expiration date from the retention period.

- If you want to code only EXPDT or RETPD, you can use this abbreviated format:

    LABEL=EXPDT=yyddd

    or

    LABEL=RETPD=nnnn

For each of the following data sets, code the LABEL parameter.

(a)   NEWCUST should have a retention period of 14 days.

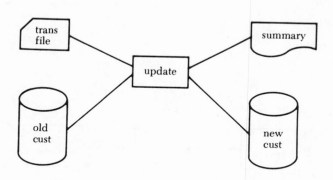

```
//NEWCUST   DD    DCB=(RECFM=FB,BLKSIZE=4800,
//                LRECL=240),DISP=(,KEEP,DELETE),
//                DSN=CUSTDSK8,
//                _____
```

(b)   NEWACCTS is the third data set on the volume. EDNEWACC should be password protected and should have a retention period of 30 days.

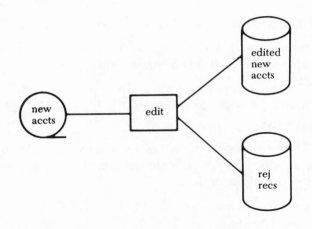

```
//NEWACCTS DD    DISP=OLD,DSN=NEWACTAP,
//               _____
//EDNEWACC DD    DCB=(BLKSIZE=12200,LRECL=122,
//               RECFM=FB),DISP=(,KEEP,DELETE),
//               DSN=EDNADSK,_____
```

- - - - - - - - - -

(a) LABEL=RETPD=14
(b) NEWACCTS: LABEL=3
    EDNEWACC: LABEL=(,,PASSWORD,,RETPD=30)

10.   COMBACCT should require a password to be written on; it can be read without one.

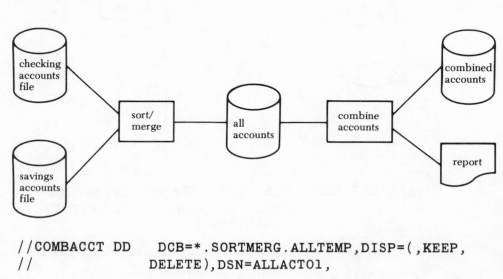

```
//COMBACCT DD    DCB=*.SORTMERG.ALLTEMP,DISP=(,KEEP,
//               DELETE),DSN=ALLACT01,
//               _____
```

- - - - - - - - - -

LABEL=(,NOPWREAD)

Review of UNIT

11.   Recall the format of the UNIT parameter, and read these statements to see how it relates to disk data sets.
   Format:

$$\text{UNIT}=\left(\begin{Bmatrix}\text{device-type}\\\text{group-name}\end{Bmatrix},\begin{Bmatrix}\text{unit-count}\\\text{P}\end{Bmatrix}\right)$$

- You must code a unit parameter for each tape or disk data set, except one that is passed from a previous step.

- Disk device types would be 2314, 2305-1, 2305-2, 3330-1, and so on.

- Disk group name is usually DISK. Your installation will create the group name.

- Avoid calling for more than one unit per data set unless you must.

Code UNIT parameters for each of the following data sets.

(a)   OLDCUST and NEWCUST must be 3330-1 type disks.

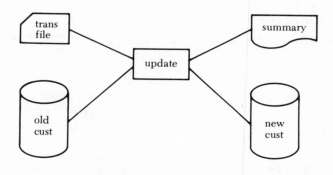

```
//UPJOB     JOB   . . .
//UPSTEP    EXEC  . . .
//TRANSFIL  DD     . . .
//OLDCUST   DD    DISP=(OLD,DELETE,KEEP),
//                DSN=CUSTDSK7,_____
//SUMMARY   DD     . . .
//NEWCUST   DD    DCB=(RECFM=FB,LRECL=240,
//                BLKSIZE=4800),DSN=CUSTDKS8,
//                LABEL=RETPD=14,DISP=(,KEEP,
//                DELETE),_____
//
```

(b)   EDNEWACC must be put on 3330-1 type disk. REJRECS can be
      put on any available disk device.

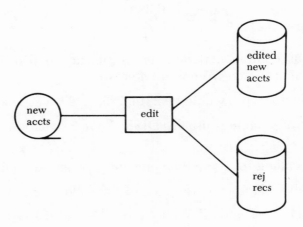

```
//EDITJOB  JOB  ...
//EDITSTEP EXEC ...
//NEWACCTS DD   DISP=OLD,DSN=NEWACTAP,LABEL=3,
//              DSN=NEWACTAP,LABEL=3,
//              _____
//EDNEWACC DD   DCB=(BLKSIZE=12200,LRECL=122,
//              RECFM=FB),DISP=(,KEEP,DELETE),
//              DSN=EDNADSK,LABEL=(,,PASSWORD,,
//              RETPD=30),_____
//REJRECS  DD   DCB=*.EDNEWACC,DISP=(,KEEP,
//              KEEP),DSN=REJDSK,_____
//
```

- - - - - - - - - -

(a) OLDCUST: UNIT=3330-1
     NEWCUST: UNIT=3330-1
(b) NEWACCTS: UNIT=TAPE
     EDNEWACC: UNIT=3330-1
     REJRECS: UNIT=DISK

12.   CHECKFIL and SAVFILE are both on 3330-1 disk. ALLTEMP and
COMBACCT may be assigned to any available disk device.
(Diagram and JCL are on the next page.)

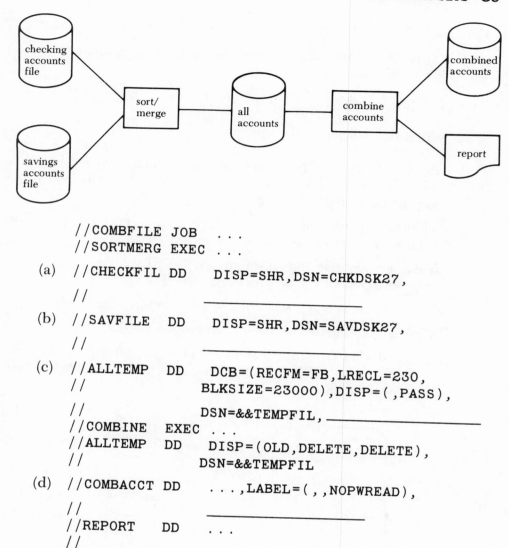

```
          //COMBFILE JOB  ...
          //SORTMERG EXEC ...
(a)       //CHECKFIL DD    DISP=SHR,DSN=CHKDSK27,
          //                  _____
(b)       //SAVFILE  DD    DISP=SHR,DSN=SAVDSK27,
          //                  _____
(c)       //ALLTEMP  DD    DCB=(RECFM=FB,LRECL=230,
          //                 BLKSIZE=23000),DISP=(,PASS),
          //                 DSN=&&TEMPFIL,_____
          //COMBINE  EXEC ...
          //ALLTEMP  DD    DISP=(OLD,DELETE,DELETE),
          //                 DSN=&&TEMPFIL
(d)       //COMBACCT DD    ...,LABEL=(,,NOPWREAD),
          //                  _____
          //REPORT   DD    ...
          //
```

- - - - - - - - - -

(a) UNIT=3330-1
(b) UNIT=3330-1
(c) UNIT=DISK
(d) UNIT=DISK

(Note: ALLTEMP in the COMBINE step does not need a UNIT parameter because it is received from the first step. The only parameters you need to code for a received data set are the "three Ds.")

Review of VOLUME

13. Recall these important facts about the VOLUME parameter. All are true for disk as well as tape data sets.

Format:

VOL=(PRIVATE,RETAIN,volume-sequence-number,volume-count,
    SER=(serial-number,...))

Abbreviated format:

VOL=SER=serial-number

- PRIVATE means the volume can't be accidentally used by other jobs, even if there's room on it; it will be dismounted as soon as the step is completed unless RETAIN is specified.
- Volume-sequence-number tells which volume in the data set you want to start with; the default is 1.
- Volume-count tells the maximum number of volumes in an output data set. (Default is 5 on tapes and 1 on disk.)
- SER tells the actual serial number that identifies the volume.

Code VOL parameters for each of the following data sets.

(a)   OLDCUST is on three volumes. The serial numbers are 16D193, 16D194, and 16D195. NEWCUST can also be expected to take three volumes.

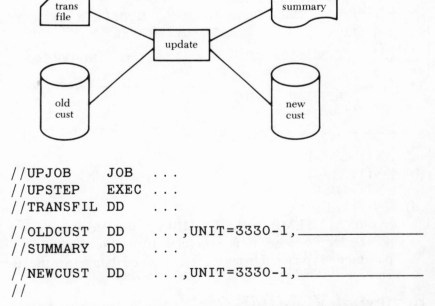

```
//UPJOB     JOB   ...
//UPSTEP    EXEC  ...
//TRANSFIL  DD    ...

//OLDCUST   DD    ...,UNIT=3330-1,_____
//SUMMARY   DD    ...

//NEWCUST   DD    ...,UNIT=3330-1,_____
//
```

(b)   The serial number of the NEWACCTS tape is 05T689.
      (Diagram and JCL are on the next page.)

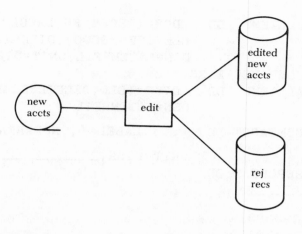

```
    //NEWACCTS DD    ...,UNIT=TAPE,_____
- - - - - - - - - -
```

(a) OLDCUST: VOL=SER=(16D193,16D194,16D195)
    NEWCUST: VOL=(, , ,3)
(b) VOL=SER=05T689

14.   The CHECKFIL volume has serial number 33D819. SAVFILE is
33D627. The new COMBACCT file should go on volume serial number
33DOAC.

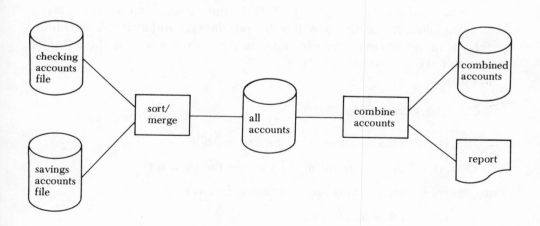

```
    //COMBFILE JOB  ...
    //SORTMERG EXEC ...
(a) //CHECKFIL DD    DISP=SHR,DSN=CHKDSK27,
    //               UNIT=3330-1,_____
(b) //SAVFILE  DD    DISP=SHR,DSN=SAVDSK27,
    //               UNIT=3330-1,_____
```

```
      //ALLTEMP  DD   DCB=(RECFM=FB,LRECL=230,
      //               BLKSIZE=23000),DISP=(,PASS),
      //               DSN=&&TEMPFIL,UNIT=DISK
      //COMBINE  EXEC ...
      //ALLTEMP  DD   DISP=(OLD,DELETE,DELETE),
      //               DSN=&&TEMPFIL
 (c)  //COMBACCT DD   ...,LABEL=(,,NOPWREAD),
      //               UNIT=DISK,_____
      //REPORT   DD   ...
```

- - - - - - - - - -

(a) VOL=SER=33D819
(b) VOL=SER=33D627
(c) VOL=SER=33D0AC

The SPACE Parameter

15.   The SPACE parameter tells the system how much room (or space) a new disk file needs. The system checks its available volumes for an unused area big enough to hold your data set.

Of the many ways to specify SPACE, the easiest is to tell the system how many blocks, maximum, will be in your data set and let it calculate how much room (in bytes) it needs. That is the only format of the SPACE parameter we will use in this book.

Format:

SPACE=(blocklength,quantity)

Blocklength is the same as blocksize in DCB.

Quantity tells how many blocks are in the data set.

For example, suppose you are creating a data set with:

Record length = 90 characters

Blocked by 5

Maximum 10,000 records

Your space parameter would be SPACE=(4500,200).

Code SPACE parameters for each of the following.

(a)   In this job, assume that NEWCUST has a maximum of 100,000
records.

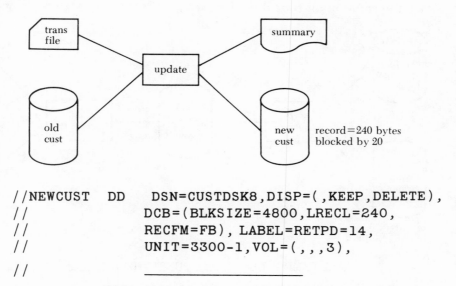

```
//NEWCUST  DD    DSN=CUSTDSK8,DISP=( ,KEEP,DELETE),
//               DCB=(BLKSIZE=4800,LRECL=240,
//               RECFM=FB), LABEL=RETPD=14,
//               UNIT=3300-1,VOL=( , , ,3),
//               _____
```

(b)   In this job, assume that EDNEWACC has a maximum of 5000
records and REJRECS has a maximum of 100 records.

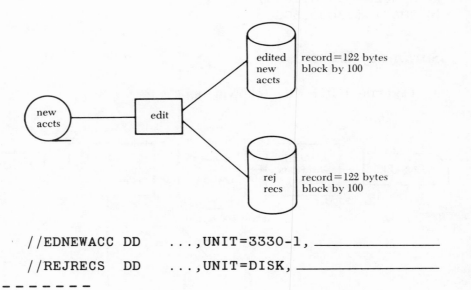

```
//EDNEWACC DD    ...,UNIT=3330-1, _____

//REJRECS  DD    ...,UNIT=DISK, _____
```

- - - - - - - - - -

(a) SPACE=(4800,5000)
(b) EDNEWACC: SPACE=(12200,50)
     REJRECS: SPACE=(12200,1)

16.   In this job, assume that ALLTEMP has a maximum of 100,000 records, and COMBACCT has a maximum of 50,000 records. Record and blocksize are the same in all four disk data sets.

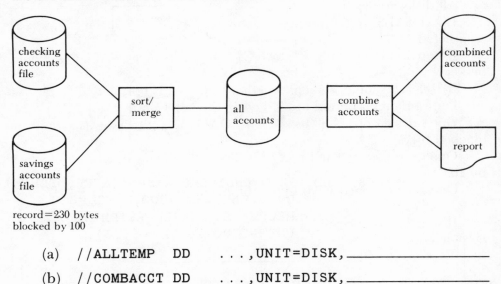

record=230 bytes
blocked by 100

```
(a)  //ALLTEMP  DD    ...,UNIT=DISK,_____
(b)  //COMBACCT DD    ...,UNIT=DISK,_____
```

- - - - - - - - - -

(a) SPACE=(23000,1000)
(b) SPACE=(23000,500)

Summary Exercise

Code the JCL for the following job.

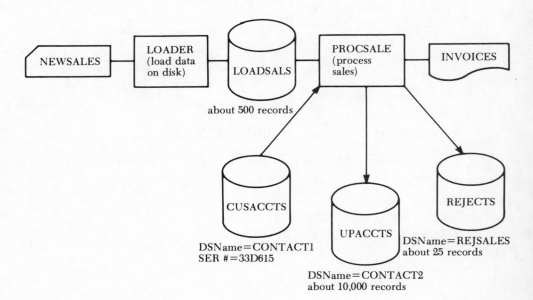

The total job time will not exceed 5 minutes; step 1 takes 30 seconds; step 2 takes 4½ minutes.

Step 1 requires 4K; step 2 requires 16K.

All disks are 3330-1.

LOADSALS is temporary; it should be deleted after the job is completed.

If step 2 ends normally, CUSACCTS should be deleted; if not, it should be kept.

REJECTS should be kept whether step 2 ends normally or not.

Put a retention period of 30 days in the label for UPACCTS.

One sales record is 80 bytes. On LOADSALS, the records should be blocked by 50.

One customer account record is 250 bytes. They should be blocked by 10.

One reject record is 90 bytes. Rejected records should be blocked by 3.

If step 2 ends normally, UPACCTS should be kept; otherwise it should be deleted.

Answer to Summary Exercise

```
//SALESJOB JOB  (PERS#3,TR-101),YOURNAME,TIME=5
//LOADSTEP EXEC PGM=LOADER,REGION=4K,TIME=(,30)
//NEWSALES DD    *
new sales records go here
/*
//LOADSALS DD    DCB=(BLKSIZE=4000,LRECL=80,RECFM=FB),
//               DISP=(,PASS),DSN=&&SALES,UNIT=3330-1,
//               SPACE=(4000,10)
//PROCSTEP EXEC PGM=PROCSALE,REGION=16K,TIME=(4,30)
//LOADSALS DD    DISP=(OLD,DELETE),
//               DSN=*.LOADSTEP.LOADSALS
//CUSACCTS DD    DISP=(OLD,DELETE,KEEP),DSN=CONTACT1,
//               UNIT=3330-1,VOL=SER=33D615
//UPACCTS  DD    DSN=CONTACT2,DISP=(,KEEP,DELETE),
//               DCB=(BLKSIZE=2500,LRECL=250,RECFM=FB),
//               UNIT=3330-1,SPACE=(2500,1000),
//               LABEL=RETPD=30
//REJECTS  DD    DCB=(BLKSIZE=270,LRECL=90,RECFM=FB),
//               DISP=(,KEEP,KEEP),DSN=REJSALES,
//               UNIT=3330-1,SPACE=(270,9)
//INVOICES DD    SYSOUT=A
//
```

chapter six

Additional Parameters for JCL Statements

You have learned the basic parameters that are necessary to create one- and multi-step jobs with unit records, disk, and tape data sets. In this chapter, we will explore a group of parameters that are sometimes, but not always, needed. When you have finished your study of this chapter, you will be able to

- Code a JOB statement including MSGCLASS, MSGLEVEL, PRTY, and COND parameters
- Code an EXEC statement including the COND and PARM parameters
- Code a DD statement for a nonexistent (dummy) data set
- Code a DD statement for an instream data set containing JCL statements

MSGCLASS and MSGLEVEL

1. When you run a job, the system automatically creates several message data sets. One data set contains the JCL statements from the job. Another data set contains system messages about the job, such as CPU time, region size, data set allocations, and so on.

You don't include DD statements for these data sets in your job; they are defined automatically by the system. But you can control these data sets somewhat with the MSGCLASS and MSGLEVEL parameters on the JOB statement. The MSGCLASS parameter sends the system messages to the designated output device. The MSGLEVEL parameter tells the system what messages to send and what to suppress. The formats are shown below.

```
MSGCLASS=output-class
MSGLEVEL=(statements, messages)
```

– Output-class is the same set of letter codes as for the SYSOUT parameter; the default is A.

– Statements is a one-digit code:

0—Write the JOB statement only.

1—Write all JCL statements, including any substitutes and insertions made by the system. This is the default.

2—Write the input JCL statements only; don't write substitutions and insertions.

– Messages refers to such system messages as CPU time, region size, "XDTASET assigned to volume serial number 24T301," JCL error messages, and so on.

0—Write no messages unless job abends. This is the default.

1—Write full system messages.

Example: MSGCLASS=D,MSGLEVEL=(0,0)

This means send system messages to the output device designated by SYSOUT class D, send only the JOB statement, and suppress normal system messages unless the job abends.

Write a JOB statement for a job named PRACCODE. Send system messages to P. Include all possible statements messages.

– – – – – – – – – –

```
//PRACCODE JOB  (PERS#3,TR-101),FERNANDEZ,MSGCLASS=P,
//          MSGLEVEL=(1,1)
```

The PRTY Parameter

2.   PRTY stands for priority, not party. Recall that the CLASS parameter tells the system in which queue (or waiting line) to place the job. The priority parameter tells the system where to place it in the queue. For example, a priority 13 job would be placed at the front of the queue; a priority 0 job would be placed at the back. Priority 5 would be somewhere in the middle.

Your installation assigns a default priority to all jobs. It's probably around 6, 7, 8, 9. You are also probably strictly forbidden to specify a higher priority than the default value without permission. There's no harm in specifying a lower one, but you may never get your job back. For practical purposes, most programmers use the default.

This is the format of the priority statement:

PRTY=priority-code

Write a JOB statement requesting queue F and a priority (you have our permission) of 10.

- - - - - - - - - -

```
//YOURJOB  JOB  (PERS#3,TR-101),JUDAVI,JOBCLASS=F,
//               PRTY=10
```

The COND Parameter

3. Sometimes you want jobsteps executed only under certain conditions. In JCL, you can specify those conditions with the COND parameter. You can code COND in JOB and EXEC statements.

JOB statement: The condition you code will be tested at the end of each jobstep; if it is true, the job will be terminated. This is *not* an abend.

EXEC statement: The condition will be tested at the beginning of the jobstep; if true, the step will be bypassed.

(a) Which parameter tests every jobstep in a job?

_____JOB COND   _____EXEC COND

(b) Which parameter checks at the beginning of the jobstep?

_____JOB COND   _____EXEC COND

(c) Which parameter will skip a step but not terminate the job?

_____JOB COND   _____EXEC COND

(d) Which parameter will terminate the whole job?

_____JOB COND   _____EXEC COND

(e) The JOB COND will terminate the job if the condition is

_____True   _____False

(f) The EXEC COND will bypass the step if the condition is

_____True   _____False

- - - - - - - - - -

(a) JOB COND; (b) EXEC COND; (c) EXEC COND; (d) JOB COND; (e) True; (f) True

4. The only thing that COND can test is *return code* from a program. The return code is a special register available to an executing program and

testable by JCL. Some programs generate return code values. For example, a system I/O routine sets a return code indicating the success of the I/O function. The calling program can test that return code and decide what to do next. If problems are encountered, the application program may decide to terminate itself after setting a return code indicating that the data was not successfully processed. Here is a sample flowchart.

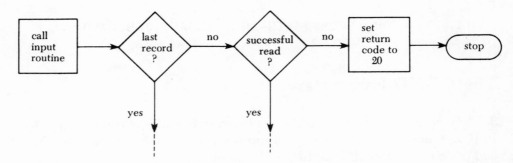

Some programs generate return codes indicating the termination status. The programmer can test the return code and control execution of later steps via the COND parameter.

COND can test for the following relationships:

GT	greater than
LT	less than
GE	greater than or equal to
LE	less than or equal to
EQ	equal to
NE	not equal to

The format of the COND parameter is as follows:

COND=(value,operator)

- Value means the value against which return code will be tested.
- Operator denotes one of the six relationships listed above: GT, LT, and so on.

Be sure to think of the value first, then the operator, then the return code when coding a COND. For example, COND=(5,GT) means "If 5 is greater than the return code . . ." This is vastly different from "If return code is greater than 5 . . ."! Code the following parameters.

    (a)   If return code is equal to 0 . . . _____

    (b)   If 4 is greater than or equal to return code _____

- - - - - - - - - -

(a) COND=(0,EQ); (b) COND=(4,GE)

You can double check your COND parameters this way: Construct a little table showing return codes, desired results as bypass or execute, and actual results.

value	52	53	54	55	56	57
desired result	byp	byp	byp	ex	ex	ex
actual result						

Then fill in the actual result for your COND. If the results don't match, fix your COND.

5. Code these COND parameters.

    (a) If return code is not equal to 16 . . .

    _____

    (b) If 8 is less than return code . . .

    _____

Watch your step on the following ones. Our questions give the return code first.

    (c) If return code is less than 10 . . .

    _____

    (d) If return code is greater than or equal to 16 . . .

    _____

    (e) If return code is less than or equal to 54 . . .

    _____

- - - - - - - - - -

(a) COND=(16,NE)
(b) COND=(8,LT)
(c) COND=(10,GE) If you said COND=(10,LT) you're wrong. That means "if 10 is less than return code" which is different from "if return code is less than 10."
(d) COND=(16,LT)
(e) COND=(54,GT)

The JOB COND

6. On the JOB statement, COND says, "If condition is true, terminate the job." The return code is tested at the *end* of each jobstep. For example, COND=(16,LE) says, "If 16 is ever less than or equal to the return code, terminate the job."

   (a) Write a complete JOB statement for a job named TRANSPRO. Include a condition that the job should be terminated if the return code is ever greater than 12.

   (b) Write a complete JOB statement for a job named CALCWAGE. The job should be continued only as long as the return code is less than 5.

- - - - - - - - - -

```
(a) //TRANSPRO JOB   (PERS#3,TR-101),FELICIA,
    //               COND=(12,LT)
(b) //CALCWAGE JOB   (PERS#3,TR-101),DUMBARTON,
    //               COND=(5,LE)
```

The EXEC COND

7. On the EXEC statement, COND says, "If the condition is true, bypass this step." The return code is tested at the beginning of the step. For example, COND=(10,GT) means, "If 10 is greater than return code, bypass this step."

Write an EXEC statement that will execute a program named PRINTLST only if the return code from the previous step is greater than 54.

- - - - - - - - - -

```
//STEPONE  EXEC PGM=PRINTLIST,COND=(54,GE)
```

8.   Write the following EXEC statements.

   (a)   The program is named ALLCHANG. This step should be executed only if the return code from the previous step is 0.

   (b)   The program is named HANGUP. This step should be bypassed if the return code from the previous step is greater than or equal to 12.

- - - - - - - - - -

```
(a) //STEPSIX   EXEC PGM=ALLCHANG,COND=(O,NE)
(b) //STEPSEV   EXEC PGM=HANGUP,COND=(12,LE)
```

EVEN and ONLY

9.   The EXEC COND allows two additional subparameters, EVEN and ONLY.

   EVEN means, "Execute this step EVEN if a previous step abended."

   ONLY means, "Execute this step ONLY if ɛ previous step abended."

Ordinarily, an abend terminates a job. But the system scans the remaining EXEC statements looking for EVEN or ONLY. If it finds one of them, it skips to that step and continues.

   Caution: The logic of an EXEC COND can get a little confusing! Usually a COND tells when to *bypass* the step; however, EVEN and ONLY tell when to *execute* the step.

```
//RESCUE   EXEC PGM=PRINTDAT,COND=ONLY
```

Here the statement says, "Execute PRINTDAT only if a previous step abends."

   (a)   Write an EXEC statement to execute a program called RE-SOLVE if any previous step in the job abends.

(b)   Write an EXEC statement to execute a procedure called
      FINDERRS regardless of whether any previous step in the job
      abended.

- - - - - - - - - -

(a) `//FINALIZE EXEC PGM=RESOLVE,COND=ONLY`
(b) `//ENDJOB   EXEC FINDERRS,COND=EVEN`

PARM

10.   Sometimes the application program you are calling to be executed will
require some data or a value to be passed to it from your JCL. If this is true, it
should be clearly stated in the documentation for the program. When you
need to pass data from your JCL to a program, you include a PARM
parameter on your EXEC statement. The format is shown below.

PARM=value

PARM is short for "parameter," and it may have a value or values in any
form, depending on the program requirements.
    For example, you want to execute a program called SELMATES. The
documentation for this program states that you must enter two dates
through a PARM—the earliest date and the latest date for records to be
selected. The format of the dates is mmddyy (all numeric). To execute
the program with the earliest date being April 1, 1949 and the latest date
being June 1, 1952, the EXEC statement would be as follows.

`//GETRECS  EXEC PGM=SELMATES,PARM=(040149,060152)`

The application program will pick up this information, store it in the correct
place, and use it appropriately in execution. The form the value takes, and
the sequence if more than one is needed, are always determined by the
program.

(a)   You want to execute a program called PRINLIST. The documen-
      tation states that you must enter (or pass, as it is usually called) a
      PARM for the number of copies of the list you want printed. Write
      an EXEC statement calling for 15 copies.

(b)   You want to execute a program called FORMAT. The program
      calls for three items of data to be passed from the JCL—(1) 1, 2, or
      3 to indicate whether you want single, double, or triple spacing;

(2) a number between 5 and 45 indicating how many lines should be printed on the page; (3) an A if you want headings and footings on each page, or a B if you want headings on top (left-hand) pages and footings on bottom (right-hand) pages. The three values are treated as positional subparameters of PARM.

Write an EXEC statement to call for triple-spacing, 45 lines per page, and option B for headings and footings.

- - - - - - - - - -

```
(a) //LISTOUT   EXEC PGM=PRINLIST,PARM=15
(b) //OUTLIST   EXEC PGM=FORMAT,PARM=(3,45,B)
```

The DATA Parameter

11.   Let's take a look now at some additional parameters for the DD statement. The DATA parameter is used in a manner very similar to the * parameter. It tells the system to treat the following records as an input data set. However, the only way to end the data set is with a record with /* in the first two columns. Therefore, the input data set may contain JCL statements—or any data starting with // in columns 1 and 2.

This is the sole purpose of the DATA parameter—to be able to enter records starting with // as data. The format is as follows.

```
//ddname    DD    DATA
```

Note that this is a positional parameter. If it is used, it must come before any other parameters in that DD statement. Usually DATA is used alone, as is *.

Suppose you want to load a JCL procedure on a library. The name of the program that will do this is LIBLOAD. The name of the data set that LIBLOAD will load is called LOADIN. It contains JCL statements and is in the input stream. Write the DD statement for LOADIN.

- - - - - - - - - -

```
//LOADIN    DD    DATA
```

The DUMMY Parameter

12.   Sometimes you want to test the logic of your application program and you don't want to bother having all the files present. So you execute your program but you mark any files that are not present DUMMY. You may also

want to suppress some of your printed output by replacing SYSOUT=class with DUMMY. Here is an example.

```
//INTRANS   DD   DUMMY
```

In executing the program, the system will ignore input/output commands for this data set. If a read is issued, the data set is treated as if the end-of-file marker had been reached.

If your data set is a new data set on tape or disk, you must still provide DCB information even though the data is not present and will not be used.

(a)   Write a DD statement for an input tape file of change of address information. In this test run, you will not have the file present; it should be treated as end-of-file.

(b)   Write a DD statement for an output disk file of reject records. The records will be 100 characters long and should be blocked by 10. For this test run, you will not need them to be written.

— — — — — — — — — —

```
(a)  //ADDRCHNG DD   DUMMY
(b)  //REJRECS  DD   DUMMY,DCB=(RECFM=FB,LRECL=100,
     //              BLKSIZE=1000)
```

Dumps

13.   You might want to make allowance for the fact that your job may abend in any step. Therefore, each step may include a data set to hold a dump. JCL allows for two types of dump data sets.

SYSUDUMP   This data set will receive a dump of the processing program storage area—where your program was when it bombed. Since this is usually sufficient information to locate the cause of the abend, most installations request or require that you use SYSU-DUMP with normal application programs.

SYSABEND   This data set will receive a full memory dump if the program abends. This includes a dump of a part of memory called the system nucleus, the processing program storage area for your job, and maybe a trace table. The inclusion of the SYSABEND DD statement in your JCL procedure automatically calls for this type to be provided.

Ordinarily, you would send either the SYSUDUMP or SYSABEND data set to the printer; however, they may be defined as tape or disk data sets if you wish your dump to be stored until a later time.

In the following job, add DD statements for dumps in steps 2 and 3.

```
//RESTORE   JOB  (PERS#3,TR-101),JNF,COND=(0,NE)
//STEPONE   EXEC PGM=LOADDATA,PARM=CARD
//INDATA    DD   *
//OUTLIB    DD   DCB=(BLKSIZE=800,LRECL=80,RECFM=FB),
//               DSN=TR506ZB,DISP=(,KEEP,KEEP),
//               UNIT=DISK,SPACE=(800,50)
//SYSUDUMP  DD   SYSOUT=A
//STEPTWO   EXEC PGM=SORTDATA
//SORTIN    DD   *
//SORTOUT   DD   DCB=*.STEPONE.OUTLIB,DISP=(,PASS,
//               DELETE),DSN=&&SORFIL,UNIT=DISK,
//               SPACE=(800,50)
```

```
//STEPTHRE EXEC PGM=PUTOUT
//SORTOUT   DD   DISP=(OLD,DELETE,DELETE),
//               DSN=&&SORFIL
//OUTPRINT DD    SYSOUT=A
```

```
//
```
- - - - - - - - - -

```
//SYSUDUMP DD        SYSOUT=A
//SYSUDUMP DD        SYSOUT=A
```

Reading dumps is difficult and time consuming, even to those who read hexadecimal. Good programmers use debugging aids in the source language and careful disk checking to solve most of their logic problems.

Summary Exercise

Write a job to execute the following.

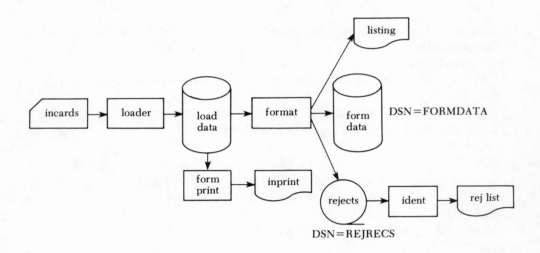

This job formats data from a unit record file into a disk file and provides a listing of the formatted data. If any data is rejected, the reason for the rejection is identified and a reject listing is printed. If any step abends, the input card images, as loaded in the first step, are printed. Get a dump for any abending step (except step 4). Request that messages be sent to the printer; you want all the messages you can get. Override normal priority and give yourself a priority of 10.

Step 1: The name of the program is LOADER. It takes a maximum of 1 minute and no more than 4K storage. You must pass it a PARM telling it how many records are in the input data and how many records will make up one disk record. The format for the PARM is

PARM=(number-in-set,number-in-record)

In this case, there are 50,000 cards in the set and it takes three input records to make up one disk record. The LOADDATA file is temporary. The loaded data should be blocked by 10. There are 240 characters in the record.

Step 2: The name of the program is FORMAT. It takes about 2 minutes and no more than 8K of storage. You must pass it a PARM telling it the number of characters in the output record. In this case ask for 218 characters. This step should not be run if step 1 produced a return code higher than 5. This is a test run and FORMDATA should be suppressed. Ordinarily, it should be blocked by 100. REJECTS tape records are 240 characters, blocked by 10.

Step 3:   The name of the program is IDENT. It takes about 2 minutes and no more than 8K of storage. It should be run only if the return code from step 2 equals 16; this means that there are rejects. The reject tape should be kept at the end of the step.

Step 4:   The name of the program is FORMPRIN. It takes about 1 minute and less than 4K of storage. It should be run only if there is an abend in the job.

Answer to Summary Exercise

```
//CARDDISK JOB   (PERS#3,TR-101),TEKNICON,
//            MSGLEVEL=(,1),PRTY=10
//LOADDISK EXEC PGM=LOADER,TIME=1,REGION=4K,
//            PARM=(50000,3)
//INCARDS  DD   *
     put input records here
/*
//LOADDATA DD   DCB=(BLKSIZE=2400,LRECL=240,
//            RECFM=FB),DISP=(,PASS),
//            DSN=&&TEMPLD,UNIT=DISK,
//            SPACE=(2400,1800)
//SYSUDUMP DD   SYSOUT=A
//FORMDISK EXEC PGM=FORMAT,TIME=2,REGION=8K,
//            PARM=218,COND=(5,LE)
//LOADDATA DD   DSN=&&TEMPLD,DISP=(OLD,PASS)
//LISTING  DD   SYSOUT=A
//FORMDATA DD   DUMMY,DCB=(BLKSIZE=21800,
//            LRECL=218,RECFM=FB)
//REJECTS  DD   DISP=(,PASS),DSN=REJRECS,
//            DCB=(BLKSIZE=2400,LRECL=240,
//            RECFM=FB),UNIT=TAPE
//SYSUDUMP DD   SYSOUT=A
//PROCREJS EXEC PGM=IDENT,TIME=2,REGION=8K,
//            COND=(16,NE)
//REJECTS  DD   DISP=(OLD,KEEP),DSN=REJRECS
//REJLIST  DD   SYSOUT=A
//SYSUDUMP DD   SYSOUT=A
//HANDABND EXEC PGM=FORMPRIN,TIME=1,REGION=4K,
//            COND=ONLY
//LOADDATA DD   DSN=&&TEMPLD,DISP=(OLD,DELETE)
//INPRINT  DD   SYSOUT=A
//
```

chapter seven

Using Utility Programs

IBM supplies to its users a number of utility programs that can be run using JCL and special control statements to accomplish many routine functions. You will learn in this chapter to use two multipurpose utility programs to handle data sets, to edit and reformat them, and to place them on other devices. These programs make the application programmer's life much easier, since they are permanently available in the system library. You will also learn how to use some advanced DISPosition processing, how to catalog your data sets for easier access, and how to uncatalog them. When you have completed this chapter, you will be able to

- Code the JCL and utility control statements to use IEBPTPCH

- Code the JCL and utility control statements to use IEBGENER

- Use an IBM utility program to copy, edit, reformat, and/or reblock records in data sets

- Specify DISPosition parameters to use the data set catalog

The special-purpose utility programs supplied by IBM reside on SYS1.LINKLIB, a system library. All are invoked by using JCL statements and controlled by using utility control statements that are unique to each utility program. Special format rules for utility control statements include the following:

Column 1 is blank.

Statement is in columns 2–71.

A nonblank character in column 72 indicates a continuation.

Begin a continuation in column 16 (JCL continuation begins in 4 through 16).

IEBPTPCH

1. Programmers often need to print out all or part of a data set. Sometimes they want a specific format for easy reading, or only certain records for spot checking, or only certain fields for comparison. Since the printing need is so common, a utility program is provided. This saves every programmer the time to write, test, and debug a simple printing program. The utility program IEBPTPCH can be used to print (or punch) any sequential or partitioned data set.

The JCL to run any program, including utilities, includes a JOB statement for the job, an EXEC statement for each step, and a DD statement for each data set required by the program. The program IEBPTPCH uses four data sets.

Input:	SYSUT1:	Contains the data set to be listed.
	SYSIN:	Contains the utility control statements for the IEBPTPCH program.
Output:	SYSUT2:	The print or card data set for the listing (LRECL defaults to 121 for IEBPTPCH, and most users use this default value).
	SYSPRINT:	For messages from the IEBPTPCH program.

The SYSIN data set contains the utility control statements for the utility. The simplest definition of SYSIN for IEBPTPCH is shown below.

```
//SYSIN     DD    *
  PRINT
/*
```

This causes the input data (from SYSUT1) to be printed (on SYSUT2) as groups of eight characters separated by two blanks. No heading is printed, no formatting is done, and all records are printed in the eight character, two blank style. This default format is very hard to interpret. The pages will be numbered in sequence, with 60 lines per page. You will see shortly how to specify formatting and other details for IEBPTPCH.

Suppose you have a data set on tape number TA287. You will need this data set (DSName is DATATAPE) for other programs later, but first you want a listing in the default format described above (each record happens to contain eight fields of eight bytes each). Code the job.

```
- - - - - - - - - -
//PRINTIT   JOB   (PERS#3,TR-101),ASHLEY
//          EXEC  PGM=IEBPTPCH
//SYSPRINT  DD    SYSOUT=A
//SYSUT1    DD    DSN=DATATAPE,UNIT=TAPE,DISP=OLD,
//                VOL=SER=TA287
//SYSUT2    DD    SYSOUT=A
//SYSIN     DD    *
   PRINT
/*
//
```

Note that PRINT does not begin in column 1, and you may place DDs in any sequence.

2.   The PRINT control statement has a number of useful options, some of which are shown below. The format of the option is shown at the left, with its explanation at the right.

STRTAFT=n   Specifies a number of input records to be skipped before printing begins. For example, STRTAFT= 10 would cause the first ten records to be skipped; the eleventh would be printed.

STOPAFT=n   Specifies the maximum number of records to be printed. (If the end of the data set is reached first, you also get a normal end.) For example, STOPAFT=50 would cause only fifty records to be printed, no matter what size the input data set.

SKIP=n   Specifies that every nth input record is to be printed. For example, SKIP=5 indicates that every fifth record is to be printed.

MAXFLDS=n   Specifies the maximum number of fields in the RECORD statement, which you'll learn about in the next frame.

MAXLINE=n   Specifies the number of lines per page. Default is 60.

These options can be used in almost any combination. Assume, for example, that your input tape contains 500 blocks of ten records each, and you have used the following control statement.

```
PRINT   STRTAFT=20,STOPAFT=100,SKIP=10,MAXLINE=50
```

Interpret this statement's effect in an IEBPTPCH run.

(a)   Which record in which block will be printed first?

_____

(b)   Which record in which block will be printed next?

_____

(c)   Which record in which block will be printed last?

_____

(d)   What line on which page will contain the last printed record?

_____

- - - - - - - - - -

(a) first record in third block (number 21)
(b) first record in fourth block (number 31)
(c) first record in 102nd block (number 1011)
(d) 50th (last) line on second page (100th printed line)

3.   Normally the user does not want output printed in groups of 8 characters. The RECORD control statement is used to specify a format or to rearrange data from the input record to the output record. The format for the RECORD statement is shown below.

```
RECORD   FIELD=(length,input-location, conversion,ouput-location)
```

- Length: number of bytes in one field in the input record.
- Input-location: beginning position of the field in the input record (default is 1).
- Conversion: any required conversion (PZ for packed to zoned). If conversion isn't needed, remember to use the comma.
- Output-location: desired beginning position in the output record (default is 1).

Example: `RECORD   FIELD=80`

This results in an 80-byte field from the input record being printed as a unit. The data is picked up starting in column 1 of the input record (the default for input location) and printed beginning in column 1 of the output record (the default for output location). No conversion is done.

Let's analyze a RECORD statement.

```
RECORD   FIELD=(5,,PZ,5)
```

   (a) How long is the field in the input record that is to be printed?

      _____

   (b) If the total input record is 48 bytes long, which bytes are occupied by the field we want to print?_____

   (c) What is indicated by "PZ" in the FIELD parameter?

      _____

   (d) In what column of the printout will the data item begin?

      _____

- - - - - - - - - -

(a) 5 bytes;
(b) 1 through 5 (input-location default is 1);
(c) The data item (field) will be converted from a packed format to zoned;
(d) column 5 (When unpacked this data item will be 9 bytes long).

4.   You frequently will want to print more than one field. IEBPTPCH allows for this, as more than one field parameter may be used; they are separated by commas. Look at the following example.

```
RECORD   FIELD=(20,1,,10),FIELD=(4,21,PZ,40)
```

This causes two fields to be printed. The first field is 20 bytes long, beginning in column 1 of the input record. No conversion is to be done, and it is to begin in column 10 of the output record. The next field is 4 bytes long and begins in column 21 of the input record. It is to be converted from packed decimal to zoned decimal (PZ) and begun in column 40 of the output record. In this example, you would have to specify MAXFLDS=2 in the PRINT statement to allow for the two fields.

Suppose you have input records in the following format.

Social Security Number	Name		Phone		Other info	
1 9	10	39	40	49	50	80

You want to produce a printout that has the social security numbers beginning in column 15 and the names beginning in column 30. No conversion is necessary. Write a RECORD statement with two FIELD parameters.

```
RECORD  FIELD=(9,1,,15),FIELD=(30,10,,30)
```

5. Suppose you want to print out a tape data set. The input tape records are in the following format.

1 – 10	11 – 40	41–49	50 – 54	55–59	60 – 61
1st FIELD ALPHA-NUMERIC	2nd FIELD ALPHA-NUMERIC	other data	3rd FIELD PACKED	other data	4th FIELD ALPHA-NUMERIC

The output lines should be in the format shown below. (Notice the fields are not in the same order.)

1st FIELD	2nd FIELD	4th FIELD	3rd FIELD
column column 5 through 16	column column 20 through 49	columns 60-61	column column 70 through 80 (convert to zoned decimal)

Now write PRINT and RECORD statements to produce a listing of every record except the first two in the above format. Use 55 lines per page, and be sure to specify MAXFLDS in the PRINT statement. Remember that a utility control statement continuation always begins in column 16; any non-blank character in column 72 indicates a continuation.

```
PRINT      STRTAFT=2,MAXFLDS=4,MAXLINE=55
RECORD     FIELD=(10,1,,5),FIELD=(30,11,,20),            X
           FIELD=(2,60,,60),FIELD=(5,50,PZ,70)
```

6.   IEBPTPCH can also print headings on a page to identify your listing. The TITLE control statement, used immediately following the PRINT statement, can specify headings, and if you use two TITLE statements, you can also specify subheadings. The format is shown below.

TITLE   ITEM=('exact title',output-location)

Example: TITLE   ITEM=('EMPLOYEE LISTING',30)

This TITLE statement defines a heading to be printed as the first line of the report, beginning in column 30.

Example: TITLE   ITEM=('NAME',10),ITEM=('ADDRESS', X
                     40),ITEM=('PHONE',65)

This TITLE statement specifies column headings. If two TITLE statements are used, the items in the second will be printed on the line following those in the first. Note the rules for TITLE statements.

One or two statements may be used (either or both may contain multiple ITEM parameters).

No more than 40 bytes per item.

The default output location is 1.

Assume you want headings as shown below. The beginning column number is shown above each heading.

```
      35
      GRADE POINT AVERAGES
10              40                65              80
STUDENT         TOTAL SEMESTERS   TOTAL POINTS    GPA
```

(a)   How many TITLE statements would you need?_____
(b)   Write the TITLE statements necessary to produce the headings.

(a) 2
(b) TITLE   ITEM=('GRADE POINT AVERAGES',35)
     TITLE   ITEM=('STUDENT',10),   X
                      ITEM=('TOTAL SEMESTERS',40),   X
                      ITEM=('TOTAL POINTS',65),   X
                      ITEM=('GPA',80)

7.   Here is a complete IEBPTPCH control statement set. The sequence of
these statements is critical—first PRINT, then TITLE, then RECORD.

PRINT   STOPAFT=200,SKIP=6,MAXFLDS=2,MAXLINE=40
TITLE   ITEM=('TEST ANALYSIS',30)
TITLE   ITEM=('TEST CODE',15),   X
                 ITEM=('DIFFICULTY',40)
RECORD   FIELD=(10,1,,16),FIELD=(6,15,PZ,42)

     Refer back to frame 1 for the IEBPTPCH data set requirements, and
write a complete job. Indicate where the control statements should be
placed. The input data set is on a 3330 disk, DSName is MASTRDSK, serial
number is UO789, and the data set should be kept.

- - - - - - - - - -

```
//UTILITY  JOB  (PERS#3,TR-101),ASHLEY
//         EXEC PGM=IEBPTPCH
//SYSPRINT DD   SYSOUT=A
//SYSUT1   DD   DSN=MASTRDSK,DISP=(OLD,KEEP),
//              UNIT=3330,VOL=SER=UO789
//SYSUT2   DD   SYSOUT=A
//SYSIN    DD   *
       control statements here
/*
//
```

IEBGENER

8.   The IEBGENER utility program can do some of the same things as IEBPTPCH, but it also has some other features, as listed below.

Input can be unit record, tape, or disk.

Output can be print, tape, or disk.

You can copy data sets.

You can edit data sets.

You can reblock data sets.

The DD statements used to run IEBGENER are the same as those needed for IEBPTPCH: SYSPRINT for messages, SYSUT1 for the input data set, SYSUT2 for the output data set, and SYSIN for the utility control statement data set.

In its simplest application, IEBGENER is run with no control statements at all; in this case, no editing or reblocking is done. The input data set is simply copied over. For example, a unit record data set can be transferred to tape by running IEBGENER with a dummy SYSIN.

Suppose you have a unit record test data set of 200 records. You need it on tape with DSName TEST33 for testing, but you still want 80 characters for each record, blocked by 10. You don't care what volume is assigned. Write a one-step job to use utility program IEBGENER to produce the test data set.

- - - - - - - - - -

```
//PRACTICE  JOB    ...
//          EXEC  PGM=IEBGENER
//SYSPRINT  DD    SYSOUT=A
//SYSIN     DD    DUMMY
//SYSUT2    DD    DSN=TEST33,UNIT=TAPE,DISP=(NEW,
//                KEEP),DCB=(BLKSIZE=800,LRECL=80,
//                RECFM=FB)
//SYSUT1    DD    *
     input records here
/*
//
```

9.   The most useful control statements for IEBGENER are GENERATE and RECORD. The RECORD statement contains FIELD parameters, just as in IEBPTPCH. The only difference is that conversion can be ZP (zoned to packed) as well as PZ. The GENERATE statement format is shown below.

```
GENERATE    MAXFLDS=n,MAXLITS=n
```

MAXLITS specifies the number of characters in literals, explained below. A few extra rules apply to IEBGENER.

- Data can be packed (ZP) or unpacked (PZ) during conversion.

- A literal (up to 40 bytes long) can be placed in the same position in each output record. Code it just after the length subparameter to replace "input location." If the literal contains any special characters such as commas or spaces, enclose it in apostrophes. For example, suppose you want to put 'NEW ACCOUNT' in columns 25 through 35 of every record created by this run. You would code:

```
GENERATE    MAXLITS=11...
RECORD      FIELD=(11,'NEW ACCOUNT',,25)
```

- SYSUT2 must have DCB information, even if it is a print data set.

IEBGENER also has options to create or bypass labels, edit several different groups of data, or handle different members of a partitioned data set. We will not cover these in this book.

input record:

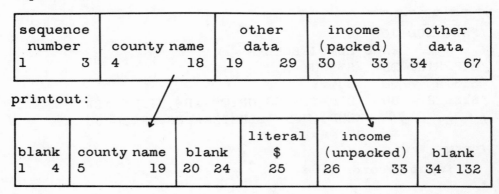

printout:

The editing shown above is to be done while printing out a tape data set, which has the DSName of EDITTAPE, serial number 24T617. The tape should be kept after printing. The printer will use a line of 121 characters. Write a complete job, including utility control statements, to accomplish the editing and printing functions.

- - - - - - - - - -

```
//EDITING   JOB
//          EXEC PGM=IEBGENER
//SYSPRINT DD    SYSOUT=A
//SYSUT1   DD    DSN=EDITTAPE,UNIT=TAPE,
//               DISP=(OLD,KEEP),VOL=SER=24T617
//SYSUT2   DD    SYSOUT=A,DCB=BLKSIZE=121
//SYSIN    DD    *
      GENERATE   MAXFLDS=3,MAXLITS=1
      RECORD     FIELD=(15,4,,5),FIELD=(1,'$',,25),     X
                 FIELD=(4,30,PZ,26)
/*
//
```

10.   IEBGENER can also be used to reblock data. This feature is especially useful when you need to create test data that has more than 80 characters per record. Here is one method for doing this.

Step 1.   Reblock the data into a temporary data set. For example, in the DCB for SYSUT2 use BLKSIZE=160. This results in an output data set with physical records of 160 bytes that is passed on to the next step.

Step 2.   Edit the data into a permanent data set. (SYSUT1 now has BLKSIZE=160; if you need 120 bytes, define SYSUT2 with BLKSIZE=120 and move only 120 positions to your final record.)

Suppose you need your test data set to be formatted as follows.

ACCOUNT NO	NAME	ADDRESS	PHONE	HISTORY	LIMIT	ORIGIN
10	30	30	10	10	6 packed	4

You have sample data of 100 records, two input records per output record, formatted as shown below.

ACCT NO	NAME	HISTORY	LIMIT	ORIGIN	15 spaces
10	30	10	11 unpacked	4	

ACCT NO	NAME	ADDRESS	PHONE
10	30	30	10

You will need a job to use IEBGENER in two steps as shown below to produce the test data file on disk.

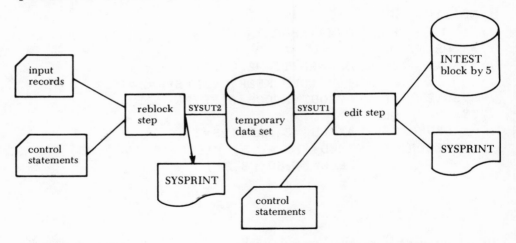

Code the first step (JCL and control statements) to reblock the data. You will need to create records of 160 bytes. Do no editing in this step.

```
//SOMENAME JOB   (PERS#3,TR-101),YOURNAME
//        EXEC PGM=IEBGENER
//SYSPRINT DD    SYSOUT=A
//SYSIN    DD    DUMMY
//SYSUT1   DD    *
     input records go here
//SYSUT2   DD    DSN=&&TEMPY,DISP=(NEW,PASS),
//               UNIT=DISK,DCB=(RECFM=FB,BLKSIZE=160,
//               LRECL=80),SPACE=(160,100)
```

11. Now write the second step. Here you will move the fields and eliminate duplications and spaces, resulting in records of 100 bytes each. You will need to specify DCB now for SYSUT1 to change LRECL from 80 to 160.

```
//          EXEC PGM=IEBGENER
//SYSPRINT DD   SYSOUT=A
//SYSIN    DD   *
  GENERATE     MAXFLDS=7
  RECORD       FIELD=(10,1,,1),FIELD=(30,11,,11),    X
               FIELD=(30,41,,41),FIELD=(10,71,,71),  X
               FIELD=(10,121,,81).                   X
               FIELD=(11,131,ZP,91),                 X
               FIELD=(4,142,,97)
/*
//SYSUT1   DD   DSN=&&TEMPY,DISP=(OLD,DELETE),
//              DCB=(RECFM=F,LRECL=160,BLKSIZE=160)
//SYSUT2   DD   DSN=INTEST,DISP=(NEW,KEEP),UNIT=DISK,
//              DCB=(RECFM=FB,LRECL=100,BLKSIZE=500),
//              SPACE=(500,20)
//
```

In the SYSUT1 statement, we specify the DCB for an input file because we want to change the record length from 80 to 160.

Advanced Disposition Processing

12. The system provides a catalog for keeping track of data sets and easily locating them when they are needed. The catalog is itself a data set that contains as records data set names and volume information. When a data set has been catalogued, it can be accessed without specifying any VOLume information. Two DISP subparameters, which can be used for normal and abnormal dispositions, are used for placing data set references in the data set catalog.

CATLG   When you are creating a data set and want it kept by the system and listed in the catalog, specify DISP= (NEW,CATLG). You may specify VOL information if you have private volumes. If you have an old data set that has not been catalogued, you can specify (OLD,CATLG) to catalog it. Once a data set has been catalogued, future references to it should not specify any VOL information.

UNCATLG   When you have a catalogued data set, and you want it removed from the catalog but kept in the system, specify DISP=(OLD,UNCATLG). If you want to delete both the data set and the catalog entry, specify DISP=(OLD,DELETE) but do not specify VOL. If you do happen to specify VOL on the DD statement, DELETE will delete the data set but will not touch the catalog entry.

Now write DISP parameters (status and normal disposition only) for the following. Include a VOL parameter if it is essential.

(a) You are creating a data set in the step. You expect to always access it by specifying a volume parameter._____

(b) You are creating a data set in the step. You don't care what volume it is assigned to, since you prefer never to code a VOL parameter._____

(c) You want to take an existing data set reference out of the catalog, but keep the data set in the system, available to you. It is on volume HP7973._____

(d) You want to remove an existing data set and its catalog reference. It is on volume PQ1720._____

- - - - - - - - - -

(a) `DISP=(NEW,KEEP)`
(b) `DISP=(NEW,CATLG)`
(c) `DISP=(OLD,UNCATLG)`
(d) `DISP=(OLD,DELETE)`

13. Following is a table of DISP parameters for catalogued data sets.

Data set	System catalog	DISP
keep	no new entry	KEEP
keep	take out entry	UNCATLG
keep	put in entry	CATLG
delete	take out entry	DELETE (omit VOL)

Both CATLG and UNCATLG may also be used for conditional dispositions. Neither is the default, but UNCATLG may result along with DELETE under the right conditions. As before, we recommend coding conditional dispositions for permanent data sets.

Refer back to the job you wrote in frame 10. Suppose you want the following to occur: If the job ends normally, put the data set reference in the catalog and keep the data set. If it ends abnormally, keep the data set, but do not put the reference in the catalog. Write the DISP parameter.

- - - - - - - - - -

`DISP=(NEW,CATLG,KEEP)`

Summary Exercise

The job described below uses IEBGENER and IEBPTPCH, and it results in a catalogued data set if the job terminates normally. Otherwise, the data set is kept but not catalogued. Write the required JCL to run the job. Include all control statements.

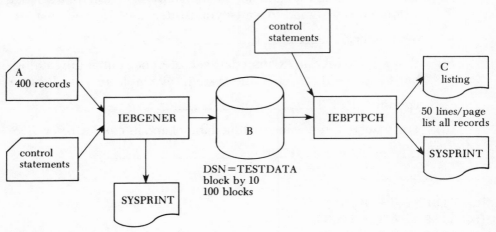

The record formats are shown below.

A (unit record)	Social Security 9	NAME 26	YR BIRTH 4	YRS EMP 2	SEX 1	RACE 1	MIL 3	etc 34

B (disk)	MIL 3	YR BIRTH 4	NAME 26	Social Security 9

C (printer)	9 name	20 MILITARY LISTING yr birth 40	50 mil

Answer to Summary Exercise

```
//NAMEJOB   JOB   ...
//EDIT      EXEC PGM=IEBGENER
//SYSPRINT  DD    SYSOUT=A
//SYSUT1    DD    *
     input records here
/*
//SYSUT2    DD    DSN=TESTDATA,UNIT=DISK,DISP=(NEW,
//                CATLG,KEEP),SPACE=(420,100),
//                DCB=(BLKSIZE=420,LRECL=42,RECFM=FB)
//SYSIN     DD    *
     GENERATE    MAXFLDS=4
     RECORD      FIELD=(3,44,,1),FIELD=(4,36,,4),      X
                 FIELD=(26,10,,8),FIELD=(9,1,,34)
/*
//PRINT     EXEC PGM=IEBPTPCH
//SYSPRINT  DD    SYSOUT=A
//SYSUT1    DD    DSN=*.EDIT.SYSUT2,DISP=(OLD,
//                KEEP,UNCATLG)
//SYSUT2    DD    SYSOUT=A,DCB=BLKSIZE=121
//SYSIN     DD    *
     PRINT       MAXFLDS=3,MAXLINE=50
     TITLE       ITEM=('MILITARY LISTING',20)
     RECORD      FIELD=(26,8,,9),FIELD=(4,4,,40),      X
                 FIELD=(3,1,,50)
/*
//
```

chapter eight

JCL in the Library

Large computer installations make heavy use of system libraries, as we discussed briefly in Chapter 1. Many system programs, many application programs, most commonly used jobs, and sets of control statements are stored in various system libraries. Many applications also require private libraries for programs and JCL. In this chapter you will learn to work with these libraries using another IBM utility program. You will learn to store JCL code in the libraries and to direct the system to a specific library.

When you have completed this chapter, you will be able to

- Assign values to symbolic parameters when you run a catalogued procedure

- Override parameters in catalogued procedures

- Include symbolic parameters in a procedure to be catalogued

- Specify default values for symbolic parameters

- Catalog a procedure

- Code and use an instream procedure

- Specify a private library using JOBLIB and STEPLIB DD statements

- Use the IBM utility program IEBUPDTE

Symbolic Parameters

1. You have learned in earlier chapters to invoke a catalogued procedure by specifying the following:

```
// EXEC procedure-name
```

This method works very well if you need to use the catalogued procedure exactly as it is written. However, many catalogued procedures include *symbolic parameters* that may be assigned values when the procedure is executed. The segment of a catalogued procedure below, which has been catalogued as SALES, includes a symbolic parameter for TIME. Notice that the symbolic parameter is preceded by a single ampersand (&).

```
//PROCSTEP EXEC PGM=PROCSALE,REGION=&REG,TIME=&TIM
//LDSALES  DD    DSN=SALESDAY,DISP=(OLD,DELETE),
//               UNIT=&UNT,VOL=SER=&VOSE1
//CUSTACT  DD    DSN=CUSTACT1,DISP=(OLD,DELETE),
//               UNIT=DISK,VOL=SER=&VOSE2
//UPACTS   DD    DSN=CUSTACT2,DISP=(NEW,KEEP),
//               DCB=(BLKSIZE=2500,LRECL=100,
//               RECFM=FB),UNIT=DISK,SPACE=(2500,4),
//               LABEL=RETPD=30
//REJECTS  DD    DSN=REJSALES,DISP=(NEW,KEEP,KEEP),
//               DCB=(BLKSIZE=270,LRECL=90,RECFM=FB),
//               UNIT=DISK,SPACE=(270,10)
//INVOICES DD    SYSOUT=A
//
```

Examine the procedure. What other parameters are also symbolic?

- - - - - - - - - -

REG, UNT, VOSE1, and VOSE2

2. The example below shows how to assign values to symbolic parameters when you run a catalogued procedure.

```
//          EXEC SALES,TIM=3,REG=64K,UNT=DISK,
//               VOSE1=OPCD17,VOSE2=MN1927
```

In the EXEC statement you specify symbolic parameters, omitting the leading ampersands, as if they were keyword parameters. You give a value to each one.

Here is another catalogued procedure, TRUPDATE.

```
//SORTSTEP EXEC PGM=SORTER
//TRANREC  DD    DUMMY
//TRANTPOT DD    DSN=&TRANTP,DCB=(RECFM=FB,LRECL=67,
//               BLKSIZE=670),UNIT=&UNT,DISP=(NEW,PASS)
//UPDTSTEP EXEC PGM=UPDATER
//TRANTPIN DD    DSN=*.SORTSTEP.TRANTPOT,
//               DISP=(OLD,DELETE)
//MASTERTP DD    DSN=MASTER,VOL=SER=&VOLSER,
//               DISP=(OLD,KEEP,KEEP),UNIT=DISK
```

```
//REJECTTP DD    DSN=&&REJECT,DCB=*.SORTSTEP.TRANTPOT,
//              DISP=(NEW,PASS,DELETE),UNIT=TAPE
//UPDATEDT DD    DSN=&NAME,DCB=LRECL=100,
//              UNIT=TAPE,DISP=(NEW,CATLG,KEEP)
//ARRNGEST EXEC PGM=ARRANGER
//REJECTIN DD    DSN=&&REJECT,DISP=(OLD,DELETE)
//LISTING  DD    SYSOUT=A
```

Don't confuse symbolic parameters with temporary file DSNs. Symbolic parameters begin with only one &; temporary file DSNs begin with two, as in &&REJECT.

Write an EXEC statement to execute this procedure, assigning values (just make them up) to all symbolics.

- - - - - - - - -

```
//          EXEC TRUPDATE,UNT=DISK,TRANTP=TRANSACT,
//              VOLSER=123456,NAME=ALLDONE
```

3.   Many catalogued procedures that use symbolic parameters assign default values to them. A PROC statement at the beginning of a catalogued procedure assigns default values to symbolic parameters.

Examine the following procedure.

```
//TRUPDATE PROC UNT=DISK,TRANTP=TRANSACT,NAME=ALLOUT
//SORTSTEP EXEC PGM=SORTER
//TRANREC  DD   DUMMY
//TRANTPOT DD    DSN=&TRANTP,DCB=(RECFM=FB,LRECL=67,
//              BLKSIZE=670),UNIT=&UNT,DISP=(NEW,PASS)
//UPDTSTEP EXEC PGM=UPDATER
//TRANTPIN DD    DSN=*.SORTSTEP.TRANTPOT,
//              DISP=(OLD,DELETE)
//MASTERTP DD    DSN=MASTER,VOL=SER=&VOLSER,
//              DISP=(OLD,KEEP,KEEP),UNIT=DISK
//REJECTTP DD    DSN=&&REJECT,DCB=*.SORTSTEP.TRANTPOT,
//              DISP=(NEW,PASS,DELETE),UNIT=TAPE
//UPDATEDT DD    DSN=&NAME,DCB=LRECL=100,
//              UNIT=TAPE,DISP=(NEW,CATLG,KEEP)
//ARRNGEST EXEC PGM=ARRANGER
//REJECTIN DD    DSN=&&REJECT,DISP=(OLD,DELETE)
//LISTING  DD    SYSOUT=A
```

(a)   Is there a default value for UNT?_____ If so, what is it?_____

(b)   Is there a default value for VOLSER?_____ If so, what is it?

_____

(c)   Is there a default value for NAME?_____ If so, what is it?

_____

- - - - - - - - - -

(a) yes; DISK; (b) no; (c) yes; ALLOUT

4.   When you execute a catalogued procedure with default values for symbolic parameters, you must decide whether to use each default value or your own. If you want to use your own, just code the parameter and value on the EXEC statement as if there were no default value.

For example, suppose you want to use the procedure from frame 3. You want to use the default values for UNT and NAME but your own value for TRANTP. You must also supply a value for VOLSER because it has no default. Here is the entire job:

```
//RUNJOB   JOB  (PERS#3,TR-101),JNF
//RUNSTEP  EXEC TRUPDATE,TRANTP=MYACCTS,VOLSER=143T69
//
```

The EXEC statement includes values for TRANTP (to override the default) and VOLSER (because there is no default). Because there are no values for UNT and NAME, the default values will be used.

(a)   Suppose you enter this statement:

```
//NEXTSTEP EXEC TRUPDATE,VOLSER=ABC123,
//               UNT=TAPE
```

What value will be used for UNT?_____ TRANTP?_____

VOLSER?_____ NAME?_____

(b)   Code an EXEC statement to run TRUPDATE with these values: UNT=DISK; TRANTP=JULTRANS; VOLSER=XYZ789; NAME=JULMASTR.

- - - - - - - - - -

```
(a) UNT=TAPE,TRANTP=TRANSACT,VOLSER=ABC123,NAME=ALLOUT;
(b) //           EXEC TRUPDATE,TRANTP=JULTRANS,
    //               VOLSER=XYZ789,NAME=JULMASTR
```

Now you have learned how to execute a catalogued procedure and provide values for some or all of the symbolic parameters.

Overriding Parameters

5.   You may wish to change a value in a catalogued procedure that is not symbolic. If the value is on a catalogued EXEC statement, you can override it by recoding the same parameter on the EXEC statement that executes the procedure.

If the value is on a DD statement, you can override it by supplying a new DD statement. On the new statement, you need code only the parameter (or parameters) that you want to override. You do not need to recode the entire DD statement. For DCB, you need code only the keyword subparameters you want to override.

For example, suppose you want to execute SALES (from frame 1) but keep the LDSALES file and send INVOICES to SYSOUT class D instead of A. Here is the job you would submit:

```
//CHANGJOB JOB  (PERS#3,TR-101),DFF
//EXECSTEP EXEC SALES
//LDSALES  DD   DISP=(OLD,KEEP)
//INVOICES DD   SYSOUT=D
//
```

The LDSALES DD statement in the execution JCL overrides the catalogued DISP parameter. The other catalogued parameters for LDSALES are unaffected. The INVOICES DD statement in the execution JCL overrides the catalogued SYSOUT parameter for INVOICES.

If you are overriding more than one DD statement, make sure to put the overrides in the same order as the catalogued statements. In the above example, the system would reject the job if the two DD statements were in the reverse order.

Code a job to execute SALES but assign CUSTACT to tape and make the REJECTS blocksize 900. (Remember: You don't need to recode the other DCB subparameters. The system will change just the one you override.)

- - - - - - - - - -

```
//EXECJOB  JOB  (PERS#3,TR-101),YOURNAME
//         EXEC SALES
```

```
//CUSTACT   DD    UNIT=TAPE
//REJECTS   DD    DCB=BLKSIZE=900
//
```

> If an override parameter conflicts with catalogued parameters, the system will suppress the catalogued parameters so the whole DD statement makes sense.

---

6.   To override parameters in a catalogued procedure containing more than one step, you must associate the stepname with the override. If you are overriding an EXEC statement parameter, you attach the stepname to the parameter keyword. For example, suppose you want to run TRUPDATE (see frame 3) but you want to set a time limit of two minutes on the second step. You would code

```
//NOWSTEP   EXEC TRUPDATE,UPDTSTEP.TIME=2
```

If you did not put the prefix of UPDTSTEP in front of TIME, the system would not know which of the three catalogued steps to apply the time limit to.

   If you want to override a DD statement, you attach the stepname to the ddname. For example, suppose you want to assign the LISTING file in the last step to SYSOUT class D. You would code

```
//THENSTEP EXEC TRUPDATE
//ARRNGEST.LISTING DD SYSOUT=D
```

   Code a job to execute TRUPDATE. Establish a time limit of one minute for the last step. Keep all data sets except the temporary ones; don't catalog any data sets. (Don't forget to override DD statements in order.)

- - - - - - - - - -

```
//EXERJOB   JOB  (PERS#3,TR-101),YOURNAME
//             EXEC TRUPDATE,ARRNGEST.TIME=1
//UPDTSTEP.TRANTPIN DD DISP=(OLD,KEEP,KEEP)
//UPDTSTEP.UPDATEDT DD DISP=(NEW,KEEP,KEEP)
//
```

7.   Instream data sets cannot be catalogued, nor can DD statements using the * parameter. Therefore, whenever you are executing a catalogued

procedure requiring instream data, you must supply the DD statement and the data at execution time.

To add a data set to a procedure, put the DD statement *after* all the override statements for the procedure. If there are more than one catalogued step, be sure to attach the appropriate stepname to the ddname.

Suppose you want to run TRUPDATE from frame 3. Override the definition of UPDATEDT in the second step so that it is a disk data set instead of a tape one. (Reserve space for 10000 blocks of 100 bytes each.) The SORTER program in the second step also needs an instream data set called LINESIN. Code the job to execute TRUPDATE. Indicate in your job where the LINESIN records would be placed.

```
- - - - - - - - - -
//YOURJOB  JOB  (PERS#3,TR-101),YOURNAME
//         EXEC TRUPDATE
//UPDTSTEP.UPDATEDT DD UNIT=DISK,SPACE=(100,10000)
//SORTSTEP.LINESIN  DD *
     instream records go here
/*
//
```

> Now that you know how to execute a catalogued procedure, let's look at how to catalog one.

Preparing a Procedure for Cataloging

8.   To get a procedure ready for cataloging, code it as a complete job first. Test that job until you know it works.

Next you can make the job into a procedure by removing the JOB statement, removing any instream data sets, removing the null statement, and inserting any symbolic parameters. Symbolic parameters on the DD statement can have the same names as the keyword parameters. For example, you can code UNIT=&UNIT,DCB=(BLKSIZE=&BLKSIZE, LRECL=&LRECL,RECFM=&RECFM), and so forth.

Symbolic parameters on the EXEC statement must not have the same names as their keyword parameters. You cannot code TIME=&TIME; you must use some other word or abbreviation, such as TIME=&TIM.

You can give the same symbolic parameter to two or more catalogued parameters if you want them to always have the same value. Use unique symbolic parameter names wherever you want to be able to assign unique values.

Give every step a name. Otherwise the user won't be able to override that step or its DD statements at execution time.

Prepare the job below for cataloging. Make all TIME, UNIT, and SPACE values symbolic. (Don't worry about assigning default values yet.)

```
//RESTORE   JOB  (PERS#3,TR-101),JNF,COND=(0,NE)
//          EXEC PGM=LOADDATA,PARM=CARD,TIME=5,
//               REGION=64K
//INDATA    DD   *
//OUTLIB    DD   DCB=(BLKSIZE=800,LRECL=80,RECFM=FB),
//               DSN=TR506ZB,DISP=(,KEEP,KEEP),
//               UNIT=DISK,SPACE=(800,50)
//SYSUDUMP  DD   SYSOUT=A
//          EXEC PGM=SORTDATA,TIME=10,REGION=200K
//SORTIN    DD   *
//SORTOUT   DD   DCB=*.STEPONE.OUTLIB,
//               DISP=(,PASS,DELETE),DSN=&&SOFIL,
//               UNIT=DISK,SPACE=(800,50)
//SYSUDUMP  DD   SYSOUT=A
//          EXEC PGM=PUTOUT,TIME=4,REGION=20K
//SORTOUT   DD   DISP=(OLD,DELETE,DELETE),DSN=&&SORFIL
//OUTPRINT  DD   SYSOUT=A
//SYSUDUMP  DD   SYSOUT=A
//
```

- - - - - - - - - -

Our changes are shown in bold face type.

```
//STEPONE   EXEC PGM=LOADDATA,PARM=CARD,TIME=&TIM1,
//               REGION=64K
//OUTLIB    DD   DCB=(BLKSIZE=800,LRECL=80,RECFM=FB),
//               DSN=TR506ZB,DISP=(,KEEP,KEEP),
//               UNIT=&UNIT1,SPACE=&SPACE1
//SYSUDUMP  DD   SYSOUT=A
//STEPTWO   EXEC PGM=SORTDATA,TIME=&TIM2,REGION=200K
//SORTOUT   DD   DCB=*.STEPONE.OUTLIB,DISP=(,PASS,
//               DELETE),DSN=&&SORFIL,UNIT=&UNIT2,
//               SPACE=&SPACE2
//SYSUDUMP  DD   SYSOUT=A
//STEPTHRE  EXEC PGM=PUTOUT,TIME=&TIM3,REGION=20K
//SORTOUT   DD   DISP=(OLD,DELETE,DELETE),DSN=&&SORFIL
//OUTPRINT  DD   SYSOUT=A
//SYSUDUMP  DD   SYSOUT=A
```

Make sure you also eliminated the JOB, null, and instream DD statements.

9.   The next step in preparing the procedure is to test it with the symbolic parameters. You can do that without cataloging it by using it as an *instream procedure.*

An instream procedure is just like a catalogued procedure except it appears in the job stream. You execute it from within the same job. The execution step must follow the instream procedure. The entire purpose of instream procedures is to test procedures before cataloging them.

Here is a sample job containing an instream procedure.

```
//TESTJOB   JOB   (PERS#3,TR-101),JDJ
//TESTPROC  PROC  UNIT=DISK,DCB=(BLKSIZE=4000,
//                LRECL=100,RECFM=FB),SPACE=(4000,1000)
//STEPONE   EXEC  PGM=IEBGENER
//SYSIN     DD    DUMMY
//SYSPRINT  DD    SYSOUT=A
//SYSUT2    DD    DSN=&DSN,UNIT=&UNIT,DISP=(NEW,KEEP),
//                DCB=&DCB,SPACE=&SPACE
//          PEND
//GOSTEP    EXEC  TESTPROC,DSN=TESTOUT
//SYSUT1    DD    *
     input records go here
/*
//
```

In this example, notice the PROC and PEND statements. They mark the beginning and end of every instream procedure and are required. The PROC statement must give a name to the procedure; here, the name is TESTPROC. Notice that name is used in the step (GOSTEP) that executes the procedure. The PROC statement might also assign default values to symbolic parameters, as this one does.

Notice also how we handled the instream data set SYSUT1. It could not be catalogued, so we added it in the execution JCL.

Test the procedure you prepared in the previous frame by making it into an instream procedure and executing it. Assign default values to the symbolic parameters at the same time. (Don't copy the procedure. Show the rest of the job and indicate where you would place the procedure statements.)

```
- - - - - - - - - -
//PROCJOB   JOB   (PERS#3,TR-101),YOURNAME
//YOURPROC PROC TIM1=5,UNIT1=DISK,SPACE1=(800,50),
//              TIM2=10,UNIT2=DISK,SPACE2=(800,50),
//              TIM3=4
      procedure goes here
//         PEND
//YOURSTEP EXEC YOURPROC
//STEPONE.INDATA DD *
      INDATA records go here
/*
//STEPTWO.SORTIN DD *
      SORTIN records go here
/*
//
```

Now you know how to prepare a procedure for cataloging. Next we'll discuss IEBUPDTE, the utility program you use to add procedures to the procedure library.

IEBUPDTE

10. IEBUPDTE is used to catalog procedures in card-image libraries. It expects to receive data in 80-byte logical records.

The utility control statements for SYSIN are different from other utility programs. They all begin with ./ in columns 1 and 2. (This is different from the control statements you used earlier.) The keyword for the statement begins after at least one space.

Normally, you need only three control statements to catalog a procedure: an ADD statement, a NUMBER statement, and an ENDUP statement.

This is the ADD statement format.

```
./ ADD    NAME=name,LIST=ALL
```

This statement specifies that you are adding a procedure. NAME gives the name you wish to use to access your procedure and LIST=ALL will provide you with a complete listing in SYSPRINT. You can omit LIST=ALL if you don't want a listing. Several other options are available for the ADD statement, but you don't need them for the basic function of adding a new procedure to the library.

This is the NUMBER statement format.

```
./ NUMBER NEW1=first-number,INCR=increment
```

This statement will ensure that your entire procedure is sequence numbered in columns 73–80, starting with the number you specify as NEW1 and incrementing by the number you specify as INCR. Numbering the statements makes it easier to update them later.

The ENDUP statement simply marks the end of the update control statements. It has no parameters.

Suppose you want to catalog a procedure named FINISH and have it sequenced by increments of 10. You would code the control statements in SYSIN as follows.

```
./ ADD NAME=FINISH,LIST=ALL
./ NUMBER NEW1=10,INCR=10
     procedure here
./ ENDUP
```

Notice where the procedure statements are placed.

Now suppose you want to catalog a procedure named RUNPAYRL. You want it sequenced in increments of 20. Write the control statements.

– – – – – – – – – –

```
./ ADD NAME=RUNPAYRL,LIST=ALL
./ NUMBER NEW1=20,INCR=20
         procedure here
./ ENDUP
```

11.   To run IEBUPDTE you also need the usual JCL statements, except that you omit SYSUT1 when the statements to be catalogued are included in SYSIN, as in the preceding examples. SYSUT2 specifies the library that will receive the new catalogued procedure. Since the libraries are catalogued data sets, you need to specify only minimum information for SYSUT2. Following is a complete example.

```
//RUNJOB    JOB  (PERS#3,TR-101),PAUL
//          EXEC PGM=IEBUPDTE
//SYSPRINT  DD   SYSOUT=A
//SYSUT2    DD   DSN=SYS1.PROCLIB,DISP=(MOD,KEEP)
//SYSIN     DD   DATA
```

```
./ ADD              NAME=PRESORT,LIST=ALL
./ NUMBER           NEW1=30,INCR=30
//PRESORT  PROC etcetera
      rest of procedure to be catalogued
./       ENDUP
/*
//
```

Notice in the procedure that SYSUT2 defines the system library. Specifying DISP=MOD ties up the library so that concurrent jobs can't access it. For this reason, many installations do not allow application programmers to update SYS1.PROCLIB. The statements for updating a private procedure library are the same as the example shown here except for the DSN for SYSUT2.

Notice also that SYSIN uses DD DATA, since the data set includes // statements. The delimiter /* is used following ENDUP.

Now code the statements needed to add the procedure SALES (last seen in frame 1) to SYS1.PROCLIB. The details of the procedure are not critical; just indicate where it would be placed. Have the numbering done in increments of 30.

- - - - - - - - - -

```
//RUNJOB    JOB   (PERS#3,TR-101),ASHLEY
//          EXEC  PGM=IEBUPDTE
//SYSPRINT  DD    SYSOUT=A
//SYSUT2    DD    DSN=SYS1.PROCLIB,DISP=(MOD,KEEP)
//SYSIN     DD    DATA
./ ADD            NAME=SALES,LIST=ALL
./ NUMBER         NEW1=30,INCR=30
//SALES     PROC etcetera
//    the procedure
//    to be catalogued
./       ENDUP
/*
//
```

12.   You can also replace a complete procedure using IEBUPDTE. The function control statement is slightly different. You must specify REPL in place of ADD.

How would you recode the procedure you wrote in frame 11 to replace the existing procedure SALES instead of adding a new one? (Code any changed statements.)

- - - - - - - - - -

```
./ REPL NAME=SALES,LIST=ALL
```

Private Libraries

13.   Most installations have private libraries in addition to system libraries. These private libraries may be used for testing programs and procedures, for storing programs or procedures, and/or for different departments or applications. These private libraries may have names similar to the system ones, except for the prefix. For example, if Judi had a complete library reserved for her testing purposes, it might be named JUDI.TESTLIB. If Ruth had a library for her procedures, it might be named RUTH.PROCLIB.

Private procedure libraries are handled much like the system ones you have been studying, with one major change. When you are expecting a program or a procedure from a private library, you must tell the system specifically where to look. You can instruct the system to search a private library first by using a JOBLIB DD (at the JOB level) or a STEPLIB DD (at the step level) to define the private library, as in the example below.

```
//JUDISJOB JOB   parameters
//JOBLIB   DD    DSN=JUDI.TESTLIB,DISP=SHR
//STEP1    EXEC  PGM=INVENTRY
```

In this example, the program INVENTRY will be searched for in the private library JUDI.TESTLIB before the system library. If there is more than one step, every program will be searched for first in the private library.

```
//stepname EXEC PAYROLL
//STEPLIB  DD    DSN=RUTH.PROCLIB,DISP=SHR
```

Here the procedure PAYROLL will be searched for first in the private library. If the next step does not have a STEPLIB card, only the system library will be used.

Notice that DISP=SHR is used here. When you are running a program or procedure, you do not need exclusive control of the library. SHR is more efficient for the installation, since many jobs can use the library at the same time.

   Assume you want to catalog a new procedure as TAXTIME in a private library called ZEUS.PROCLIB. You want it sequenced in increments of 5.

   (a)   Write a complete job to catalog TAXTIME.

   (b)   Write the statements necessary to run the procedure using all defaults established in it.

- - - - - - - - - -

```
(a) //FEDJOB    JOB  (PERS#3,TR-101),DUMBARTON
    //STEP1     EXEC PGM=IEBUPDTE
    //SYSPRINT  DD   SYSOUT=A
    //SYSUT2    DD   DSN=ZEUS.PROCLIB,DISP=(MOD,KEEP)
    //SYSIN     DD   DATA
    ./ ADD         NAME=TAXTIME,LIST=ALL
    ./ NUMBER      NEW1=5,INCR=5
    //ZEUSPROC PROC etc.
    //     statements to be catalogued
    ./ ENDUP
    /*
    //
(b) //RUNJOB    JOB  (PERS#3,TR-101),DUMBARTON
    //          EXEC TAXTIME
    //STEPLIB   DD   DSN=ZEUS.PROCLIB,DISP=SHR
    //
```
(Note: You could have used JOBLIB right after JOB instead of STEPLIB after EXEC.)

Summary Exercise

This summary exercise incorporates much of what you have learned as you have worked through this Self-Teaching Guide. You will code a job to use an IBM utility program to produce a disk data set from instream input. Then you will code a complete two-step procedure that processes that disk data set. Then, you will write the execute JCL to run the two-step procedure instream. Finally, you will prepare a job to catalog the procedure, then write execute JCL to run the catalogued procedure.

(a) Assume you have a set of about 2000 cards as an input data set. You need the first 38 and the last 5 positions formed into a 43-byte record on a disk. Block the records on disk by 20. Ddnames are indicated in the diagram below. Create job and step names as needed. Feel free to refer back to earlier portions of this book. The index will direct you.

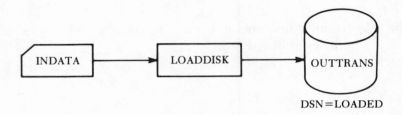

OUTTRANS should be kept if the job is successful, otherwise deleted. Code this job.

(b) A two-step procedure is diagrammed below.

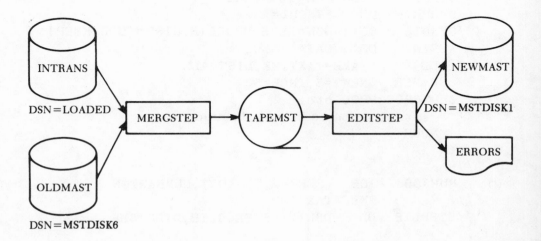

INTRANS: This is the OUTTRANS data set from part (a); it was placed on volume serial number PT7171. It can be deleted only if the step runs successfully.

OLDMAST: This is a catalogued data set and should be kept.

TAPEMST: This is a temporary data set with the same DCB information as INTRANS.

NEWMAST: This data set should be catalogued if the run is successful, otherwise kept. It has the same DCB information as INTRANS and TAPEMST. You should allow for a maximum of 6000 records and ensure that the data set is kept at least 90 days.

ERRORS: This is a standard print data set; it should use a line length of 45.

Now code the job.

(c) Now write the JCL to run your job from part (b) as an instream procedure.

(d) Modify your answer to part (b) so that the procedure is ready to be catalogued. Allow the INTRANS data set volume number to be entered when the job is executed. Set the retention period for NEWMAST to 90 days as the default, but use a symbolic parameter so the user can override it. Add the statements necessary to catalog the procedure and number records using increments of 10.

(e) Now write the JCL to execute SUMMARY, using volume PT7171 for INTRANS and a retention period of 90 days. For this run, OLDMAST is an instream data set.

Answers to Summary Exercise

```
(a)  //LOADJOB   JOB   (PERS#3,TR-101),YOURNAME
     //ONLYSTEP  EXEC  PGM=IEBGENER
     //SYSPRINT  DD    SYSOUT=A
     //SYSUT2    DD    DSN=LOADED,DCB=(LRECL=43,
     //                BLKSIZE=860,RECFM=FB),DISP=(NEW,
     //                KEEP,DELETE),UNIT=DISK,
     //                SPACE=(860,100)
     //SYSIN     DD    *
         GENERATE MAXFLDS=2
         RECORD   FIELD=(38,1,,1),FIELD=(5,76,,39)
     //SYSUT1    DD    *
          input records
     /*
     //

(b)  //SUMMARY   JOB   (PERS#3,TR-101),YOURNAME
     //STEPONE   EXEC  PGM=MERGSTEP
     //INTRANS   DD    DSN=LOADED,UNIT=DISK,
     //                VOL=SER=PT7171,DISP=(OLD,DELETE,
     //                KEEP)
     //OLDMAST   DD    DSN=MSTDISK6,DISP=(OLD,KEEP,KEEP)
     //TAPEMST   DD    DSN=&&TEMP,DISP=(NEW,PASS),
     //                UNIT=TAPE,DCB=(RECFM=FB,LRECL=43,
     //                BLKSIZE=860)
     //STEPTWO   EXEC  PGM=EDITSTEP
     //TAPEMST   DD    DSN=&&TEMP,DISP=(OLD,DELETE)
     //NEWMAST   DD    DSN=MSTDISK7,UNIT=DISK,
     //                DCB=*.STEPONE.TAPEMST,
     //                DISP=(NEW,CATLG,KEEP),
     //                LABEL=RETPD=90,SPACE=(860,300)
     //ERRORS    DD    SYSOUT=A,DCB=BLKSIZE=45
     //

(c)  //FINALJOB JOB   (PERS#3,TR-101),YOURNAME
     //PROCNAME PROC
             EXEC for STEPONE through ERRORS DD statement
     //         PEND
     //         EXEC PROCNAME
     //

(d)  //CATJOB    JOB   (PERS#3,TR-101),YOURNAME
     //          EXEC PGM=IEBUPDTE
     //SYSPRINT  DD    SYSOUT=A
     //SYSUT2    DD    DSN=SYS1.PROCLIB,DISP=(MOD,KEEP)
     //SYSIN     DD    DATA
     ./ ADD      NAME=SUMMARY,LIST=ALL
```

```
./ NUMBER NEW1=10,INCR=10
//SUMMARY   PROC RET=90
//STEPONE   EXEC PGM=MERGSTEP
//INTRANS   DD   DSN=LOADED,UNIT=DISK,
//               VOL=SER=&SER,DISP=(OLD,
//               DELETE,KEEP)
//OLDMAST   DD   DSN=MSTDISK6,DISP=(OLD,KEEP,KEEP)
//TAPEMST   DD   DSN=&&TEMP,DISP=(NEW,PASS),
//               UNIT=TAPE,DCB=(RECFM=FB,LRECL=43,
//               BLKSIZE=860)
//STEPTWO   EXEC PGM=EDITSTEP
//TAPEMST   DD   DSN=&&TEMP,DISP=(OLD,DELETE)
//NEWMAST   DD   DSN=MSTDISK7,UNIT=DISK,
//               DCB=*.STEPONE.TAPEMST,
//               DISP=(NEW,CATLG,KEEP),
//               LABEL=RETPD=&RET,SPACE=(860,300)
//ERRORS    DD   SYSOUT=A,DCB=BLKSIZE=45
./ ENDUP
/*
//

(e) //RUNJOB    JOB  (PERS#3,TR-101),YOURNAME
    //          EXEC SUMMARY,SER=PT7171
    //STEPONE.OLDMAST DD *
          OLDMAST records here
    /*
    //
```

Why JCL?

JCL is a language by which the programmer communicates with the operating system. It can be *thought of* as a conversation (even though it is not really conversational, as you shall soon see) that goes this way:

Programmer: I have a job for you.
Operating System: What's its name?
P: EMPMASTU
OS: Who shall I charge it to?
P: The Personnel Department.
OS: What hardware configuration do I need?
P: Two tape units, three disk units, and one printer.
OS: I'll make the following assumptions unless you stop me.
    (1)   You'll use virtual memory.
    (2)   All output messages will be printed on standard computer paper.
    (3)   I will output the following types of messages:
        (a)   system messages
        (b)   JCL messages
    (4)   This job has a priority of 7.
    (5)   Your job needs a region of 64K.
    (6)   Your job will take no more than 10 minutes.
    Is that OK?
P: Yes.
OS: What's the first jobstep?
P: I want you to execute the program named UPMAST.
OS: I'll make the same assumptions about this jobstep. OK?
P: Yes.
OS: What data sets are required?
P: First is INTAPE. It's on one reel of tape. It has standard labels. Check for a tape serial number 24T316. Check the label for the name EMPCHGS. It's an input data set, mount it on a 2400 tape drive, and you should keep the reel with the data after this step is completed.

OS: What's the next data set?
And so on.

Actually, JCL is more like a memo that the programmer sends to the operating system. The programmer supplies all the information without waiting to be asked. If the programmer leaves anything out, the operating system will send back an error message and will not process the job, or will make some incorrect assumptions and botch it.

TO: OS
FROM: Programmer
RE: Job EMPMASTU
Charge to: Personnel
Use normal assumptions
Job Class: F
First step: Execute program named UPMAST
               Use normal assumptions:
               Data sets:
               (1) INTAPE
                    (a) use one reel on 2400 drive
                    (b) standard labels
                    (c) serial number 24T316
                    (d) label name: EMPCHGS
                    (e) use as input
                    (f) keep it after the jobstep
               (2) And so forth.

In reality, the programmer must code the "memo" in the only form that the OS can read, JCL.

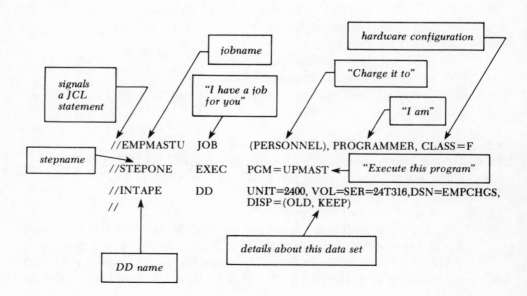

Glossary

Batch: When a whole group of input data is processed in one run, as opposed to online.

Buffer: A memory area set aside to hold an input record before it is read or an output record after it is written.

Byte: A storage area usually containing eight bits (binary digits), used to store a single character.

Catalogued procedure: JCL statements that have been stored in the Procedure Library and can be referenced by name.

Compile: To translate a program written in a high-level language, such as COBOL, into machine code; in the process, error messages and warnings may also be produced. See also: compiler program, link edit, object code, source code.

Compiler program: A program, developed and supplied by the system manufacturer, that translates source code into object code. See also: compile.

Data control block: A block in storage that tells the system how to read or build a data set; it contains such information as block size and record size.

Dump (memory dump): An output of all data (valid and nonsense) currently stored in memory for the program being processed; usually done when the system has reached an impossible instruction and must stop processing (i.e., abend).

EDP: Electronic data processing; the use of electronic equipment to read, manipulate, store, and output business or scientific information.

Execute: To run a load module, with data files, on the computer.

Hardware configuration: An assemblage of input, processing, and output equipment.

High-level language: A programming language that is close to everyday people language but requires translation into machine language to be executable.

Input stream: A sequence of unit record data being read by the operating system's main input reader.

Label record: A record associated with a file (tape or disk) that identifies the file for the system; it contains such information as the name of the file.

Library: A partitioned data set containing programs or catalogued procedures that can be referenced by name.

Link edit: To create a program that can be executed by the system (called the load module); this involves filling in copied or called modules, resolving address references, and so on. See also: link editor program, load module, object program.

Link editor program: A program developed and supplied by the system manufacturer, that translates an object program into a load module. See also: link edit.

Literal: Data supplied by the program itself, rather than by the input files; titles and headings for reports are frequently supplied as literals.

Load module: A program that has been compiled and link edited and is ready to load and run.

Master file: A file that contains all of a company's records for one application; for example, companies usually maintain master files of their employees, their customer accounts, and their product inventories.

Object code (object program):   A program that has been translated into machine language; it must still be link edited before it can be executed.

Operating system (OS):   A set of programs, developed and supplied by the manufacturer, that control the basic functioning of the computer; JCL is the language used to communicate with the operating system.

Operator: In a conditional test, the type of comparison that should be made— greater than, less than, equal to, not equal to; also, the person who runs the machine.

Override: To supplant data or instructions stored in the system (such as a default value) with your own.

Packed decimal: For numeric data, to represent each external digit with only four internal characters, instead of eight; this means that you can save room by packing two digits into each byte, plus one half byte for the sign; this can be done only with numeric data. See also: byte, zoned decimal.

Parameter: An item of information whose value can be set and changed; a variable.

Queue: A waiting line; the operating system maintains queues of jobs for each jobclass.

Return code: A two-byte, numeric value that can be set by a program and will be maintained after the program ends; JCL procedures can test the value of the return code field using the COND parameter.

Run: Execute; when a program is loaded into memory and control is passed to the first instruction, the program is being run.

Sequence number: A number that shows where an item belongs in an overall sequence of items.

Sort: To put in sequence; common sequences are ascending alphabetic, descending alphabetic, ascending numeric, and descending numeric.

Source code (source program): A program written in a programming language; a source program must be translated before it can be executed.

Spooling: Saving unit record files on disk to avoid making the system wait for I/O operations to be completed.

Subparameter: A part of a parameter; for example, in a date, the month, the day, and the year can be subparameters.

Virtual storage (VS): A means of extending memory capacity by segmenting programs and data and storing internally only those segments currently in use.

Zoned decimal: Normal storage of decimal numbers with one digit per byte; alphabetic data is also stored in zoned format. See also: packed decimal.

Index